HEART TO HEART CONVERSATIONS

Attain the power to Aspire & Inspire

HEART TO HEART CONVERSATIONS

Attain the power to Aspire & Inspire

JAWAHAR SUSHILA
BHAGWANDAS DODANI

PRABHAT
PAPERBACKS

Publisher
PRABHAT PAPERBACKS
4/19 Asaf Ali Road, New Delhi–110 002
Ph. 23289555 • 23289666 • 23289777 • Helpline/ 7827007777
e-mail: prabhatbooks@gmail.com • Website: www.prabhatbooks.com

Edition
First, 2022

Price
Three Hundred Rupess Only

ISBN 978-93-5521-064-7

Printed at
AMSONS, Sahibabad

HEART TO HEART CONVERSATIONS
by Jawahar Sushila Bhagwandas Dodani

Published by **PRABHAT PAPERBACKS**
4/19 Asaf Ali Road, New Delhi–110 002

ISBN 978-93-5521-064-7

₹ 300

Acknowledgements

This book "Heart to Heart Conversations", is dedicated to my dear Mom who is not only my Guru but also like a God to me. I have not seen God but I can imagine God in form of my mother who would have loved and care for me just like my mom did and she continues to do even more after she left me in July 2019.

She always inspired and aspired me and we always had Heart to Heart conversations.

I am changing my name to Jawahar Sushila Bhagwandas Dodani. Sushila is my mom's name. I would like to thank my dad who took care of my mom and always loved and inspired me.

I am also thankful to my wife Amrita who is mother of my two great kids and dedicated her life to raise them.

I am so proud of my two amazing kids who keep me going and both make me very proud.

My daughter Shannon at a young age is such a great psychologist and very successful and doing amazing things.

My son Nik is also very successful. At a very young age he is very successful actor in Hollywood and his latest achievement is that he is in Broadway.

All the gratitude to my four super sisters and an older brother and their kids who love me very much.

Thanks and appreciation to Rajesh Aggarwal and Sadaf Khan without them this book would have been just a dream.

They came up with great questions for heart to heart conversations and I responded straight from my heart without any preparation and without knowing the questions in advance.

As a CEO of Dodanis World, Jasbir Singh Bhatia did a super work to get this book happen. Jasbir has been my dear friend for 45 years. I can't forget to give attribute to my two dear friends for last 20 years in USA, Nagesh Gidwani and Samarth Mohan Pathak with whom I have Shared and learned many lessons of life.

Then we have Dishanu Rajput, Who converted our zoom conversations in Hindi to an English script for the book she did an amazing Job in a very short time. Shalvi Agarwal also did editing and Bhakti Shah gave input for the book.

The others who have played a key role in the book are Sayan Roy, Navjot Singh, Parth Acharya, Pranav Joshi, Darshank Kannada, Shivani Singh, Ravi Nath Pandey, Amreek

Kumar, Sumit Singh, Jaydeep Barad & Siddhi Sathiya Barad.

My vision for this book is to engage with readers with love and passion and do my best to inspire and aspire them like my mom did and change their life in a way that they are in love with themselves first and are eager to pass on love to others with zero expectations - Love Zero.

Testimonials

1. We don't always need to be inspired or motivated, sometimes we just need to slow down and reconnect with ourselves.

   This book gives you a power of connecting yourself with soul and humanity.

   I know it will be life changing book for every reader

With best wishes

Anchor Siddhi Sathiya Barad

M.D of dodani's world TV

Vice President of Creative hands of India

2. I have known Jawahar S B Dodani for over 20 years.He has always been bubbling with entrepreneurial ideas. His mind is like a boiling cauldron of different thoughts, some conventional, some unconventional and some uniquely innovative. He extrapolates unique lessons from each new venture he has done which adds a greater dimension of his understanding of the world. I have not read the full script of the book, but knowing him he must have some great insight of his journey of life.

– **Dr. Nagesh Gidwani**

Dentist & Author of Dadfucious

3. "Some books really could change the way you lead your life, and this book beautifully encapsulates the importance of love and humanity. Amidst everyone striving to be perfect and having a toxic

trait to be famous and materialistic, this book is a gentle reminder to stay grounded no matter where you are in your life, to look on the positive side. One can surely take away life-changing and an inspiring messages in between the pages of this book"

Best Wishes;

– **Niyati Mehta**
Founder | CEO,
#Be The Change, Ahmedabad

4. "Heart to Heart Conversations" is a book full of emotions and comes with some real life lessons.

   In the world where everyone is running for perfection, this book taught us to be real to ourselves & real to the world. It inspires us to be happy & keep others happy & motivated with our positive aura.

Heart to Heart Conversations is a great book, with positive life transforming messages.

Best Wishes

– Dr. Sabiha Rahmani

Professor, Government Girls PG College

Legal Advisor, Family Court,

U.P. Police, Banda U.P.

About the Authors

Jawahar Sushila Bhagwandas Dodani

Mr. Jawahar Sushila Bhagwandas Dodani is the founder of Dodanis World, Meri Maayi, Uplift1mom.org and many other entrepreneurial ventures. He recently launched Studio 'Creatives Hands of India' in Ahmedabad promoting Indian Artists around the globe. He is also launching Dodanis World TV soon. Born and raised up in Ahmedabad, he is now settled in America since last 40 years. Jawahar was first to bring Pizza in Ahmedabad in 1976 by the name Jasuben Pizza and it is still loved by people in Ahmedabad. He is also a Real Estate broker with eXp Realty dealing in land and known as Land Guru in Arizona USA. He is constantly working for the upliftment of human life. He is also a publisher of Chalo Amdavaad, a book dedicated to Heritage City Ahmedabad. He is also working to bring Chalo Gujarat book in 2022. Jawahar believes in LoveZero, Love everyone with Zero Expectations.

– Jawahar Sushila Bhagwandas Dodani
Founder / President
Dodanis World
Phone: (480)200-7127
Jawahar@DodanisWorld.com
8989 E Via Linda, Suite 117A,
Scottsdale, Arizona, USA

Rajesh Aggarwal

Rajesh Aggarwal is known as Business Owner, Coach, Motivational Speaker & Personality Development Expert.

His coaching methodology has helped many individual, Business owners , organisation & Entrepreneurs to achieve their desired Goals.

He is working in this field since 1993. He has been referred as Dr.Destiny by Business Today

His You Tube video has more than 215k subscribers worldwide.

Rajesh has spent more than 6000 hours in the field of Personal & Business Success.

His Easy to understand & Quick to apply techniques are almost like reading many books in 90 minutes.

In his coaching ,Rajesh makes sure to provide a process which reduces the time of achieving any Goal.

His Virtual & Live sessions are available in English, Hindi & Bangla.

Till now , his Live sessions have took place in 92 cities of India including America, Dubai, Bangladesh, Nepal & Thailand.

He is an author of six books, Rajesh Aggarwal Success Journey started as Courier

Pick Up Boy at the age of 19 yrs and went up to Training Director, Entrepreneur & Founder of Rebirth Academy

Rajesh takes maximum 90 minutes to Two hours group sessions on Talking Skills, Mindset, People Handing Skills, Public Speaking & Personal Branding.

He also provides one to one Virtual Coaching.

For more details visit www.rajeshaggarwal.net

Let's travel a New Thinking Journey with Rajesh Aggarwal

Sadaf Khan

Ms. Sadaf Khan is an advisor of Real Estate in eXp Global India and heading Maayi Real Estate in Delhi NCR, powered by eXp. She is also a Chief Team Builder in Dodanis World.

She started her career as a banker but her calling was also in training and academics so when she got an opportunity, she switched to education sector.

She became a faculty at one of the top universities.

During her stint she also enrolled herself in a PhD in Human Resource in order to work in field of Training Consultation more effectively.

At a young age, she has achieved a lot. She is a well known writer, performed at National TV News Channel Show "Arz Kiya Hai" 24*7 JK News. She regularly performs at local events and has also performed at an International organisation event, "One Billion Rising".

Her social work life started since college days. She is a President of voluntary organization "Agaaz" which was founded in 2015. She is also the founder of "Say It Out Loud", a mental health initiative. Sadaf's core belief goes by this famous quote by Roy T. Bennett "Great things happen to those who don't stop believing, trying, learning and being grateful".

– **Sadaf Khan**
Chief Team Builder
Dodanis World
Mobile: 8826596030
E-mail: sadaf@dodanisworld.com
New Delhi, India

Jasbir Singh Bhatia

Jasbir Singh Bhatia is business consultant specially in Hospitality Industry since 1992. PMC is Always First requirement of any Project as his expertise decide success of Project.

Excellence in Business and Business Up Lifting Service for retaining customers are Core subjects of his Coaching.Every project's first need is a consultant. Expertise of consultant decides the future/success of the project. Jasbirsingh is also a Hospitality coach. His core target in business is "Excellence in Business " and as a coach he gives training for uplifting business services. He teaches how to develop customer in to your free sales person for uplifting your business and much more. He is developing properties with team and turn the properties in a successful model. Not only this Jasbir Singh is working as Real Estate Advisor in Ahmedabad by name Maayi Real Estate powered by Exp.

– Jasbir Singh Bhatia
CEO, Dodanis World
Mobile: 98250 50246
E-mail: Jasbir@DodanisWorld.com
3rd floor,Centaur Complex
Opp.Bank Of Maharashtra
Vijay Cross Road, Navrangpura,
Ahmedabad-380009, Gujarat, India

CONTENTS

Session 1

One Life to Live, Live Like no Other

Introduction

Sadaf Khan: Hello everyone, I am Sadaf Khan and your host for the show "HEART TO HEART CONVERSATIONS". Today we'll be talking about life and its different perspectives, approaches and interpretations. We have a very special person joining us to talk about it. Allow me to introduce to you all Mr. Jawahar Sushila Bhagwandas Doodani. He is the founder of Dodanis World, LoveZero, uplift1mom.org and many other entrepreneurial ventures. Born and raised in Ahmedabad, he is now settled in America since the last 39 years. He is also a Real Estate broker dealing in land with this he is constantly working for the upliftment of human life.

Now for the second guest of the show, also known as thought transformer - Mr. Rajesh Aggarwal. A person who can transform the thoughts of any person he meets through his unique approach of questions and logical deduction. He is someone who questions the old mindset and creates a new mind frame, something he has been doing for the last 27 years.

On the thought of life, I have something to ask Jawahar Sir. I am curious to know why you have two middle names. Anything special or significant about it?

Jawahar S.B. Dodani: Sure Sadaf. First of all, I wanted to thank you and Mr. Rajesh Aggarwal for doing this. I will request him to give his introduction and he will also talk about "Heart to Heart Conversations". What is the purpose? What is the vision? What is the objective?

And now about my middle name, you must have heard that generally in India we have a tradition to have the father's name or Husband's name as a middle name. We live in a patriarchal frame of society.

Sadaf Khan: Yes, I am aware of it.

Jawahar Dodani: This middle name after marriage, why should it only be a guy's father's name or husband's last name? Why?

This question came to my mind very recently, like a couple of years ago when my mother passed away. I can go on and on and tell you all about her and how she was just not a mother but a perfect human being and I can also prove it to everybody. However, the truth is that a mother is someone without which this world cannot survive in peace. Without a mother, I don't know what will happen to this world, or humankind for that matter? Without a mother, what will happen to kids as well as adults like myself? I was 64, when my mother passed away two years ago, yet she always treated me the way she would treat me when I was a kid. It is truly said that for mothers, their kids are forever their children regardless of how old they become.

I would like to share some quotes on mothers that have inspired me. Like Abraham Lincoln said that "All that I am, or hope to be, I owe to my angel mother" and another gentleman shared that for everything I am today, my mother's love showed me the way". One can find thousands and thousands of quotes on mother and each one of them is so true. And it's not just a recent phenomenon, thousands of years ago when Rama Rajya was there or any religious scripture or anything like that, they all had respect for their mothers and their mothers have gone beyond everything for their children. Ram left for exile because of his mother and father.

So when my mother passed away I had no teacher (Guru). I believed in God because my mother was a believer. If anything good happened to her, she always gave credit to God, and if something bad happened or she suffered, she always said that it was all God's plan. She believed that whatever happened was according to God. But I was not a believer. I did not go to temples to pray, however I do have an idol, the Lord Ganesh, which a friend of mine brought for me.

So I did not believe in God but I love people who believe in God because people who truly believed in God like my mother knew how to live life. Now the people who don't believe in God will deny it. They will say the other people don't know how to live life but no, it is not like that.

Another thing is that I tried to find mentors (Gurus) in my life but could not. I did see my mother mentor me in many ways all through her life, so one day I decided that she is my mentor (Guru), she is my God. This thought occurred when I was sitting and filling up an application or a form or probably talking to someone who was asking my name. Without realising, I filled Jawahar Bhagwandas Dodani in the name column. That's when I realized why?? Why is my mother's first name isn't there in my middle name? So I suddenly thought of doing Jawahar Sushila Dodani but then my father also loves me. He is 84 and still cares and takes care of me till date. Fathers do love kids. Don't get me wrong but not like a mother. Mothers have something special. So I added my mother's name along with my father's name as my middle name. It was to recognize my mother, to recognize my mentor (Guru), to recognize my God and that is how the two middle names came up.

Sadaf Khan: Thank you for sharing Sir. It is really wonderful and touching. It is said that

God could not be everywhere, and therefore he created mothers. I feel that without mothers, this world is not going to be a better place.

Now coming to Rajesh sir, I wanted to know if you feel the same or you have any perspective on what Jawahar Sir said.

Rajesh Aggarwal: Thank you very much Sadaf for hosting this show and acting as a bridge between us. I also want to thank my "brother from another mother", yes and my good friend and business partner - Mr. Jawahar Dodani Sir. I met Jawahar Sir just a month back, I think around 10th of March and since then, it has just been an addition after addition in our chemistry. I can't see a scenario of having any possibility of a minus between me and him at all. And thanks to you Sadaf and the whole team of Heart to Heart Conversations, as love is the central theme of our relationship so it has to be in plus.

Now, coming back to Jawahar sir's thoughts on mothers, so you see I lost my mother a few years back. The last 15 days before her demise have been a bittersweet memory for me. In those 15 days she would serve me the same food that she used to serve me when I was a child or a young boy. The taste was the same, the flavors were the same and I was wondering why this was happening? I intuitively felt that something was going to happen and suddenly within 15 days we lost her. I completely agree with Jawahar Sir that there is no substitute for mothers. Mothers are just irreplaceable.

Sadaf Khan: Thank you sir and I would also like to add something to it. When I told my mother that this was happening, she was so curious to know each and every detail. She was very excited and happy to see me like this. I think she was more excited than me. I realised that this is what a mother is, someone who loves you and your work from the bottom of her heart. Thank you so much for this discussion and thoughts, sir.

Question 2

Sadaf Khan: With this, I have one more question.

Rajesh Aggarwal: Yes, go ahead.

Sadaf Khan: Sir, Everyone has a different perspective about life, some crave money, some crave love, and for some people, life is still a mess that they are not able to manage. According to you, what is your biggest achievement in life till now? Jawahar sir it would be great if you can also say something. Rajesh sir, can we start with you if that's ok.

Rajesh Aggarwal: Well, I would like Jawahar sir to say first and then I will end with my version. So let's hear from Jawahar Sir first.

Jawahar Dodani: I am 66 years old and have two wonderful kids. My daughter Shannon was a psychologist in San Francisco, but moved to Arizona about a year ago in December 2019, just before Covid happened.

She was wondering during the pandemic, how she would practice, though she has a California as well as an Arizona license. Her business is to help people and people need desperate help. Teenagers, young kids, adults, she just started with the intention of helping and her practice is going crazily well. Nonetheless, it is not the practice I wanted to talk about but the help she is to others is what I wanted to share. The cases and the stories are confidential but she has told me generic stories about people and I am amazed by her work, her spirit and her thought to never be defeated.

My son, his name is Nikhil but he goes by Nik. When he was growing up, he was an introverted kid till he was 8-9 years old. My wife and I wondered and worried to some extent about him. So we decided to put him into an acting class at the age of 10-11. He started loving the class and enjoyed it a lot. So much so that now he is a very successful actor and has done many great things in L A. And not just acting, he is also a standup comedian and is also producing his show. He is only 26 and the show has been written by him and his friends. They have sold the show to ABC Studios and are trying to find their final destinations on big platforms like Netflix etc.

The reason I talked about my children's achievements was to bring home the point that I have always taught them - Every action has its consequences. But when they started getting success at an early age, I added one more sentence "Be humble". No matter how much success you will get but if you are not humble then that success is a waste, it is all for no good. However, if you have success and you are humble then people are going to love you and you are going to love people. It is just going to be an amazing journey. And surprisingly, they have done that.

I think it's a story for another session. Coming back to your question, I want Mr. Rajesh to give his views.

Rajesh Aggarwal: Sure Sir. Sadaf talked about life and Jawahar sir explained beautifully about his kids and family and shared his perspectives. Let me now share the answer to the question that you have asked - what is the purpose of these sessions or this series of heart to heart conversations?

First of all, different minds meet means started with when we met – roughly around the 10th of March 2021.We exchanged ideas, points of view and connected with each other. We kept on liking each other's point of view and eventually in this process we discovered that two individuals and now Sadaf included can come up with so many ideas based on our personal lives and experiences. And through these experiences, we can help to transform the lives of people. So basically the purpose of different minds meet is just a conversation between a few individuals about their life and experiences. Whether it is good or bad, positive or negative, we are not going to evaluate or judge but go with the flow. We are going to be as authentic as possible and in this process, we hope that people will pick up some good ideas and neglect the bad ones. So the whole concept is to change their experiences through our experiences.

This is the first initiative and we have decided to take on many topics like life, relationship, money and so on. The entire idea is quite simple. How can we change the experiences of people about this wonderful life? The reason we are saying this is because our wish to build an empire based on love, which is also the central theme for all our endeavours.

Question 3

Sadaf Khan: Wow, what an initiative sir!

My next question is based on the different emotions we go through in life - negativity and positivity. Sometimes we feel dejected, hopeless, struggle a lot and try to give up on life very easily. It is dependent on how well we are trained to cope up. But if we talk about the millennials or people of this generation, we see that they lose hope very soon, very quickly.

So what should be the techniques or tactics of coping up with these negatives or hard situations? Can you please shed some light on this as we need to talk about these aspects in our society so that it would help many of us?

Jawahar Dodani: You know Sadaf, this question that you asked is very close to my heart because of my daughter. As I mentioned, she daily counsels young people on aspects of ending one's life or losing hope. However, I am not a trained or certified psychologist. I don't want to act like one as it would mean like I am belittling a respected profession which my daughter is part of. So I would like to caution my audience and request them that if they know anybody who is in such a situation and going through challenges, please seek professional help or help them to seek it. The professional help will facilitate them to evaluate, determine, plan and recommend their situation and its solution. I have realised the criticality of professional help, thanks to my daughter.

My input though is going to be coming from experience and unprofessional. Sometimes, what I feel is missing is love. When I say love it overlooks things such as young or old, age, color, sex, caste or anything that would divide or alienate.

Everybody needs some people in their life with whom they can share everything without having any fear of being judged and still be loved and respected by them. We do our parents and siblings and they will always be there to love but sometimes we can't share with them openly. A close friend or acquaintance can facilitate such a type of sharing and help them come out of their issues or trouble.

The other thing, like my father, sometimes he feels low, for instance, when he misses my mother. As he is old now and he feels that when my mother was alive he took her for granted like any traditional Indian family. Now when he thinks about his past, he realizes how wrong he was.

I always suggest a technique to many people which is to stand in front of a mirror and look at your life regardless of your age. You will see the many positive things that you have done for others like family members or friends, and recollect those things. I sincerely believe that everybody has done well in their life and when you remember them, it creates a positive image in your brain. When you help others it goes into the subconscious mind and stays there whenever we think about it, it comes up. To conclude this segment, I would say that in difficult situations, one can either get professional help or they can go to the person who loves them with zero expectations like their mother, siblings or close friends. Like I share my concerns with my close friends.

Rajesh sir, what do you think? What would you like to add?

Rajesh Aggarwal: I agree with what you said. Nonetheless, I would like to add one more point that we need to accept ourselves. Acceptance is a must, when you try to reject yourself the way you are, or you evaluate yourself from others' perspective then self-esteem goes down. The moment you start accepting, your self-esteem will rise and you will feel very comfortable in dealing with any situation.

Sadaf Khan: I believe today's session is going to be very helpful because this is what everyone is facing - the lack of acceptance and self-love. Thank you So Much!

Question 4

Sadaf Khan: On to our next subject. It is the age of technology. Everyone is running towards fame and bothered about the number of views or friends who like their posts on social media. Sometimes, we judge our lives based on our social media. In this rat race, somewhere, we are losing true friendships and relationships. So how should we keep our personal and professional life balanced? Social media is important but to what extent and how much.

Jawahar Sir, you have a lot of experience in this matter, can you share.

Jawahar Dodani: Well, I would like to first share with the audience that this communication or conversation has been designed by Rajesh Sir and Sadaf, so I don't know what questions they are going to ask and thus I have not prepared any script. Whatever I say is coming directly from my heart and what I feel about it. So apologies if I sometimes go off topic or add some experience to explain.

I would like to start by accepting that there is a generation gap between my father, me, and my kids. Its three generations and whatever my parents saw and experienced is different from us. My mother was good with the changes around her, accepted them and that's why she understood and listened. I love her so much. But my father is still a traditional conservative man, he follows what his generation taught him, and is not able to accept the changes that he encounters with time. I hope to be like my mother around my kids and grandkids.

This generation gap is going to stay and we need to work around it. Like social media is a new age blessing or boon, depending on how we see it. It is important for today's generation. I still like paper over mobile applications, however my son does things differently. He made a to-do list for me on the phone but I haven't even opened the app. You Sadaf are also in the same age group as my kids and might be more inclined towards social media versus traditional methods of connecting. I am not against social media, I do use Facebook once a week and my son signed me up on Instagram which I have hardly used. I prefer the old ways of meeting up and talking. I am more used to calling than texting and would prefer catching up over tea than chatting. People of today's generation have a different way of doing such things. They do like to meet up with their friends, like my daughter is upset as due to COVID she can't go out and meet up. However, with the use of social media, people tend to connect over there instead of meeting in person. There is a lot of negative content too easily available on social media which attracts and engages. The likes, subscribe and number of followers can also be looked at in two ways – positive and negative. This is true of most things in life as well and it is up to an individual how they want to look at it. For example, technology has made it easy to do business with whatsapp and social media makes it easy to connect to a wider audience.

So, I leave this decision to every individual as they choose to view it. If you like it then enjoy it and if you don't then that is also okay. That's my thinking about social media or technology.

Sadaf Khan: Rajesh Sir, you change everyone's mindset, through your work. Would you also share your take on balancing a personal and professional life in today's era?

Rajesh Aggarwal: So, as Jawahar Sir said, I would like to reiterate that social media is a necessary evil. Right now we are doing this conversation that will go on various social media platforms. So we can say that we can't breathe without social media in today's times and it's a fact that we have to deal with. Now, coming to the second point, are we a victim of social media, or are we a master of social media? We can very easily determine it through our behaviour, if we are a victim, then whenever I am posting on social media I will be looking for acknowledgement and validation. But if I am using social media for the growth and development of my business and profile then I will be the master of social media. I will not discredit social media but would like to say that use social media, but don't get used by social media.

Jawahar Dodani: Sadaf, I would like to ask something. We are talking about self-love, balancing professional and personal life and social media. So, why don't you as a young person give your input on this?

Question 5

Sadaf Khan: Sure and my next question is also related to it. If I talk about myself then living life to the fullest is more important to me and that has been my life's agenda. Though sometimes we are caged as a human because of social pressure, as many times we have to meet the expectations of family and relatives. In such cases, we lose the happiness that we wanted. When we start thinking that I have to do this to make my family happy and please society, we end up killing our own happiness. This is the dilemma that is faced by people in my age group or the upcoming generation of what one should really do. As Jawahar sir said that self-love is very important. But sometimes we are tied up in social norms and end up compromising on our happiness.

Jawahar Dodani: I was having a discussion with Rajesh Sir about my life and I told him the same thing that you are saying right now. You are young and you have this view that I even after 66 years of my life also have. All my life and even today, before I do anything I have this thought that what will my kids, family members, society, friends, and clients think about it. There is no doubt that you have to think about these things but sometimes in life, you have to see what is best for you and move forward as long as you are not hurting someone. If you respect and love people then it is fine to do what you think is best. It is also written in Shri Bhagwat Gita "Karm Karo, fal ki chinta mat Karo", you should do your best without worrying about the result. We should not think about others' perspectives of us. If we do our best in life then we should let God decide what other people think about us. We live our life for others which is a shame, so I am glad if you are learning and thinking about this at such a young age. I hope that after getting to my age, you enjoy your life without thinking about hurting other people. You cannot hurt other people and that is the first condition you have to keep for yourself.

Sadaf Khan: Rajesh Sir, I think you will also have some views. You probably might be dealing with this problem many times, can we have your views on it?

Rajesh Aggarwal: Can you rephrase the question again so that I can have a fresh mindset about it?

Sadaf Khan: Basically if I talk about myself, I want to live my life to the fullest but sometimes I or people in my age group are pressured to meet society's expectations and give up on their dreams. What do you think about that?

Rajesh Aggarwal: Okay, got it. You know Sadaf, I have been trained by the world's best trainers, masters, or mentors. And not only training, but I also stayed with them as I wanted to see if there is any similarity or difference in what they are saying and what they are doing. So my passion was to be with them. I asked some very private questions which no one asked them and this also led them to become my friends. Earlier we were teacher and student but later we became friends. So one of my trainers, I will not share his name, but he shared something beautiful which I still remember. It may be a joke perhaps but I think he was serious. He said,

"Listen Rajesh, suppose you are married and if your wife doesn't like a particular vegetable but you like it, in that case, what are you supposed to do? Have that vegetable outside your home and keep it to yourself so that your wife can be happy?" I believe there comes a point in life where you have your private life and space and you also have to balance your family life so you have to use your intellect and find a way to your personal happiness or else you will die as you will not have your own life. This is the only answer that comes to my mind as of now.

Sadaf Khan: Sir, you have made it very clear that we have to choose our happiness but as Jawahar Sir stressed without hurting others.

This has been a very fruitful discussion, but I have been also pondering on how you both think. You have mentioned the basic idea of these sessions but I still want to know what will be the change in the mindset of people according to you both, post these conversations?

Rajesh Aggarwal: I think let's hear from Jawahar Sir. Though he gave me and you the credit for designing everything, it is not the fact. The fact is this whole idea even the title 'Heart to Heart Conversations' was initiated by him. Of course, we did the logistics part. So, let me go to Jawahar Sir and let him answer the question and I will perhaps add to it.

Jawahar Dodani: You know this is an interesting turn of events right now, especially the question you asked. I don't think Rajesh Sir, me or you are trying to teach anybody. It's not a lecture. On 'when different minds meet', we just talk about our life and what we think about it. The thing that I would like to get out of this is that whoever listens to this should live their own life, the life they want to live without hurting other people.

Suppose there is another Jawahar, or Sadaf or an artist listening to this. They will listen to the life stories which we three are going through and they will be like if Jawahar did this, then I can also do it. So in the future sessions, we are just going to openly talk about almost everything, what we do, what we like, what we enjoy! The idea is not to change other people, but for them to accept themselves, love themselves. This is why I desire that the people become so in love with themselves, love with their inner circle that they start loving even strangers- that's the ultimate goal. Out of this series, one thing is sure that people will learn how to love themselves, their inner circle, and eventually even strangers. The inner circle can be their family, kids, parents, spouse, siblings or friends. Thanks to this series, I have got to know Rajesh Sir since a month, Sadaf since two months and myself for 66 years.

I know Rajesh Ji and Sadaf so well in such a short period and I also know myself. We love to love ourselves and that's why we are here in front of you talking about our life and experiences.

Sadaf Khan: Thank you, sir! I would also

like Rajesh sir to answer and throw some light on it so that someone who is struggling probably comes out of it.

Rajesh Aggarwal: I agree with what Jawahar sir just said, we are just initiating the idea that self-love is not selfishness. Accept yourself the way you are. I was reading a book in the afternoon where the author was telling, 'my only teaching is to help people to think, I don't want to give any thinking, and I just request them to think'. Everyone has a brain, they can think and with this conversation, if we allow them to think, then I hope this would have touched their heart somewhere.

Sadaf Khan: Yes sir, I think this was the basic idea about self-acceptance and self-love that makes everything change in a positive way. As Jawahar Sir said, we are not here to change the mindset. So I too hope that maybe somewhere some other Sadaf Khan is watching this and probably relate to it. She might think about life, what it is and probably make some positive changes in her life. If that happens then the purpose of this initiative is fulfilled.

Before ending, I want to add that sometimes we might give up on life. I am still trying to understand life and make my career. I also wanted to end as things were uncertain and I did not know which path to take. But then life also surprises you with uncertain happiness. Like when I met Jawahar Sir on 28th December 2020 and then I still remember the call that I got, it was 8 am and on 1st January 2021, I joined as a member. This is the uncertain happiness I was referring to. One never knows from where one's life is going to change and what is waiting for one ahead. All one can do is never give up, practice self-love and trust that one day you are going to shine.

Thank you so much Jawahar sir and Rajesh sir for this wonderful session.

Jawahar Dodani: Sadaf, one last thing, I started this session with my mother and I want to end it with my mother. Look at this, it is my parents' picture, somewhere in their middle age. They look so good and young and I just love them.

So on that thought, I have a humble request to my audience. If you do not talk to your parents for whatever reason, please pick up the phone and call them, or go and visit them and please do take care of them. Just like I added my mothers' name in my name, you also have the choice to do this more often. Let's bring our mothers into the limelight. I am not talking about doing exactly what I did but let's show this patriarchal society that mothers are equally important. Personally, I think mothers are more important than fathers, but at least give them equal recognition all around the world. Thanks, I would like to now end this session by paying my respect to my mother. I love you, mom and I know you are watching me (tears rolling down).

Sadaf Khan: Thank you for sharing your emotions with us. This is how we perceive these sessions to be – unfiltered and raw. The idea is not about perfection, but reality. Thank you!

Rajesh Aggarwal: Thank you!

Jawahar Dodani: Thank you! I appreciate Sadaf and Rajesh Sir. I would also like to acknowledge Parth Acharya who is recording these sessions and would be creating the social media for it. Thank you very much Parth.

Sadaf Khan: Thank you Jawahar sir! Thank you Rajesh Sir! Thank you Parth. And a big thanks to the audience for listening and appreciating us.

❑

Session 2

Love Zero: Love with Zero Expectations

Introduction

Sadaf Khan: Hello everyone, I am Sadaf Khan and your host for the show "HEART TO HEART CONVERSATIONS". This is our second episode and we will be talking about one of the most important feelings - LOVE. Joining us today is Mr. Jawahar Sushila Bhagwandas Doodani. He is the founder of LoveZero, uplift1mom.org and many other entrepreneurial ventures. Born and raised in Ahmedabad, he is now settled in America since the last 39 years. He is also a Real Estate broker dealing in lands with this and is constantly working for the upliftment of human life.

The other guest with us, also known as thought transformer is Mr. Rajesh Aggarwal. A person who can transform the thoughts of any person he meets through his unique approach of questions and logical deduction. He is someone who questions the old mindset and creates a new mind frame, something he has been doing for the last 27 years.

I welcome both the esteemed guests. Please note that this session is going to be unfiltered and raw.

So, to start off, we all have different perspectives about love, like for some people love is everything and for others it is just a part of life. It is based on an individual's perception and has different meanings for each one. So Jawahar Sir, how will you define love? We want to know your perspective.

Jawahar Dodani: Namaskar everyone, Sadaf, Rajesh Sir, and everyone who is watching this show. Well, I would like to first share with the audience that this communication or conversation has been designed by Rajesh Sir and Sadaf, so I don't know what questions they are going to ask and thus I have not prepared any script. Whatever I say is coming directly from my heart and what I feel about it. So apologies if I sometimes go off topic or add some experience to explain.

So, love! As you shared with Sadaf, there are different perspectives or types of love. Like the love of mother, friends, siblings, girlfriend-boyfriend, husband-wife and many more. But I think the true definition or the definition of love according to me is respect. Love is nothing but caring for each other. Love is not between two-persons only, love can be for anyone. Forget about people, I have my son's pet dogs, I don't even call them dogs, we call them our kids or they are like my grandkids. I love them. Probably our showing of love might be different but ultimately it all comes down to respecting and caring. If we don't respect and care for other people, no matter in whatever relationship you are, we can't call it love.

Sadaf Khan: Rajesh sir, would you please share too? How will you define love?

Rajesh Aggarwal: First of all, thank you Sadaf and I also would like to extend my gratitude to my brother from another mother, Dodani sir. I really feel as if he is my big brother. Our relationship started with a very petty client and faculty relationship, converted to friendship and now we are family. I never had a brother in my life and always wanted one, Dodani sir came into my life and fulfilled that wish on mine.

Jawahar Dodani: Thank you! You see, this is what love is. This is the true definition of love. When you get a feeling for somebody like now between the three of us, we know each other for a few months. Like I know Sadaf a little bit longer (like 5-6 months) and Rajesh sir around 3-4 months. But what Rajesh sir said and what Sadaf tells me many times, this is what true love is. You can call it friendship, whether you know a person for years or for a few months, when there is a connection between people then that can be a form of love.

Sadaf gave a brief introduction about Rajesh sir, but if you Google him up you will get to know how important a person he is in India. I am in America and I never thought I would build a relationship like this with somebody that big in India. It was possible because of our love, respect and the care for each other.

Rajesh Aggarwal: Thank you Dodani sir. I am honoured. Let's address Sadaf's question now. Sadaf you know when I was young, by young I mean biologically, like in my twenties, my definition of love was different. I had just crossed teenage so one can understand what kind of definition of love I would have? When I crossed my thirties, my definition changed and then when I crossed my forties, the definition changed once again. Now, at the age of fifty, my definition has changed and is somewhat in line with what Dodani sir has said. Love is giving, either by your smile or by your good wishes or by loving somebody from a distance. There are some situations, where you love somebody not by remaining close but from a distance. So, to summarize it, if you are in a giving mode in any way with either respect, care, or concern, you are in love.

Sadaf Khan: Wow, that's insightful.

Question 2

Sadaf Khan: With this, comes my next question. Most of the time in life, we experience many kinds of feelings. As we grow up, we understand that feelings are very important but do you think love should be considered as the most important feeling? Is it important to keep love at the highest point or are there other feelings too? Do you think that keeping love at the highest point is right?

Jawahar Dodani: You know, there is a show of Amitabh Bachchan in India - Kaun Banega Crorepati, which has the options of lifelines. Whenever a lifeline comes into play, he calls somebody for the answer. So I am going to call my mother for this answer.

As you know, my name is Jawahar Sushila Bhagwandas Dodani, and Sushila is my mother's first name and Bhagwandas is my father's first name. My mother passed away in 2019, she was 83-84 years old. When I look back at her life I realise that my mother lived such a great life. How was she able to do that? Everyone loved her, I never came across a person who talked negatively to her. I always thought that it was because she was always nice to them or was it because she loved everybody? What was in her?

If I can decipher the answer to it then I would have answered Sadaf's question.

It's a very difficult question to describe how she lived her life. There was love, respect, and care. She was emotional too, but she never took things to heart. I am trying very hard to become like her, wherein I don't take anything to heart. If somebody gives love or not. I don't mean that you have to control your feelings.

I don't. I start crying sometimes and I will not be surprised if I tear up in this show. What it means is that we should not control or stop our feelings but we should not attach ourselves to others or any feeling. I think my mother did that perfectly, she loved and cared for everybody but I don't think she was attached to anything. She had an attachment with my father but even that was superficial because of the social obligation that he was her husband. She was attached with kids but because of the relationship between mother and child. Honestly, she was truly attached to only one person and that is God. I think other than that one relationship, she wasn't attached to anybody. I will not say that she faked her emotions, she was capable of doing her best with everyone else. However, for God, she had total faith and belief.

Whenever she was sad, in deep sorrow or suffering, she used to remember God and say, whatever God will do she will accept. When there was some great news like if she had grandkids or the wedding of any close relative or if something very good happens in the family, she would always say everything is approved by God. I think feelings are important as they display love and I will come to the same point that if you respect and care for someone then it is the best way to show your feelings.

Sadaf Khan: Thank you sir for the wonderful answer. With this, I pass on the question to Rajesh Sir. What are your views on it, should love be considered as the highest feeling?

Rajesh Aggarwal: What else can I share,

Sadaf? As Dodani sir shared about his mother that she was always in love 24*7. You know my guru's guru (mentor's mentor) used to say love is real, rest is not. Love is the only reality whether we understand it today, tomorrow or the day after tomorrow. I feel at this point that the only purpose of us coming on this planet is to love. We are born for love, the only reason that we exist as the highest creation in the world is to love. So, the purpose of living on this planet is to spread love.

Many people suffer from different negative emotions and pass through a negative phase, even though I have passed through it. I am not any God, or any special child of God, he created me like everyone else. But I prayed to God as to how to live my life in love for a long time. Thus I worked on myself and am still working at present too. Sometimes I get angry, I get negative emotions but the purpose is not to live in the negative phase but to turn it into positivity. As it is said that a single ray of sunlight is enough to remove all the darkness.

So, the question you asked about love being the highest emotion, I don't see anything else except it.

Sadaf Khan: So true, as you said that love is all you need.

But, nowadays, we see that people give a lot of importance to money, status, work, and somewhere or the other they do not consider love as life but only keep love as a small part. They just think of it as an obligation that they have to fulfil. So, love gets a little time and all the time is focused on work, money, and status. What are your views on this?

Rajesh Aggarwal: Thank you for this wonderful question. I appreciate it. I wonder sometimes if we will take our breath in part-time too. Like I will breathe later but first I should complete my work. So, whether you are into money, power, position, or status, all should have love in it. It's your ambition, I don't want to interfere with it. But if those ambitions are joined with love inside, it would be amazing. Now, I would request Dodani ji to talk about Love zero.

If you have zero expectations and you have love to give then you can go behind money, status, or power. But that power should have love as power without love will make you corrupt and violent. So, to summarise this I would like to say that love cannot be a part-time job. It has to be there with you for 24 hours just like you breathe.

Sadaf Khan: Thank you, sir! Joe sir, I know you have a lot of experience in this area and we also want to know about LoveZero from you.

Jawahar Dodani: You know when you say I have a lot of experience, I will not completely agree with it. If I look at my life, I would live it differently than what I have lived. I will not deny that I did run behind money and I am still running behind it. Power comes due to money. Whether you can say power or fame, every human being likes it. Honestly, even doing this video is a part of it and there might be other reasons too but money and fame can't be denied. I also made a lot of mistakes in my life, in terms of neither giving love nor receiving it.

Money is important and you do gain some power with it. However what Rajesh sir shared about LoveZero is also the truth. I saw this website some 3-4 years back and purchased it. I did also spend a lot of money to buy the site. Love Zero is to love everyone with zero expectations. The day you start doing this then life will be wonderful. However, I don't think it addresses your question. So let me share a true incident from my life.

I will share a true story. I usually tell everyone that I love them. For example, if I tell Sadaf that I love her without clarifying what it means then people will say: What the hell is he talking about. The same thing happened when I went to the bank. I would say I love you to the employees, but before saying this I used to tell them about Love Zero. They repeated back to me, I love you, Joe. So, when you have zero expectations you can express love to everyone.

Normally, people do not do this, because they are afraid about what people will think about this.

So, coming back to money, power, and love. One will understand its relevance only with passing time. For example, if one reads the last letters of Steve Jobs, one can probably comprehend it. Jobs had everything when he died, billions of money, was the founder of Apple but what he shared through his last words was so different from his actual life. The phrase "I love you" is so common that we take it for granted. But we should not. Just like we work very hard the entire day to earn money, in the same manner if you want to earn love then you have to work upon it daily. You have to do things because you can feel that the person in front of you is giving love and respect to you. That's my answer to your questions.

Sadaf Khan: Thank you, sir, with this I want to add something to this question. When I was discussing this with my mother, she told me that it is written: "Khuda hi Mohabbat hai aur mohabbat hi khuda hai". And this sums up everything in all. I told her that these are some heavy words that you are saying. But she laughed and said that this is the reality. So moving forward on the same idea here is my next question.

Question 4

Sadaf Khan: Nowadays, many times when a relationship fails, we start running away from love. This relationship is not necessarily related to a partner but it can be with your friends, siblings, or parents as well. After one heartbreak, people come to conclusions like, 'No, we are not going into any relationship', 'we will be practical' and 'we will be stone-hearted.', especially the millennials. Sometimes people also face depression and trauma. I want to ask your take on how to overcome a situation after a relationship breaks. Jawahar Sir, what are your views on this?

Jawahar Dodani: You know Sadaf, I know the answer for this question will be very different because of my personal life. I have never openly talked about my personal life and only a few close friends and kids know about it. Today for the first time I am sharing publicly that I am divorced. I got a divorce after 34 years of marriage. If I look back at my life, I can think of many possibilities like maybe my relationship would not have worked as it was meant not to be or maybe if I would have lived a different life, it could have worked. I don't know the answer yet but I think it's a very difficult situation. In the case when it doesn't work with a spouse then you can take divorce, but what if it doesn't work between children and parents or siblings or close friends, what should be done?

For instance, Rajesh Ji is here, in the future if something happens between us and it doesn't work well, then how to break off. All these relationships are tied to each other so closely. A person can overcome difficulty in breaking up with a spouse, there is sadness for sure but both sides can deal with it. According to me the most difficult situation is between kids and parents. I remember my elder brother has not talked with my parents for the last 15 years. He lives in America and he is the eldest among 7 siblings. However, my mother, my goodness, never complained about him but she always missed him.

Whenever I went to Dallas, she told me to knock on his door and I did so every time. My mother came to America 5 or 6 years ago for the wedding of my sister's daughter. Somehow I managed to call my brother to the airport. Luckily, he came to meet her but again vanished. He did not come to the wedding. Sometimes I feel that my mom came to America for the wedding definitely but deep down she wanted to see my brother one last time. Also, after that, they never met. I think this is the toughest relationship.

I have gone through some tough times in my marriage and both my children have also gone through tough times. We share a bond but I have only one fear that I would never go away from my kids. I pray to God each day for that day to never come as I will not be able to face that situation. I love my kids and don't know how they will respond to this when they listen to this recording. But, I never want to face a situation in my life where my kids won't talk to me for any reason. Personally, that will be most hurtful for me. Will I be able to face it? Yes! But still, it will be extremely difficult and very depressing. I have seen people going through depression when there is failure in relationships. I understand it as I have seen it closely when my daughter went through it or other close acquaintances. But I strongly also believe that jaise subah hoti hai Raat ke baad, in the same way, there is something that we will gain even after failure. Life teaches us lessons and what we learn is amazing. One does feel bad about it but in the end, you have to move on as well.

Sadaf Khan: Thank You, Sir! You are right, we indeed learn from our failure. When we fall then only do we get the strength to stand up and walk again. Rajesh Sir, would you like to share your views on the same?

Rajesh Aggarwal: Ek Sher Suna deta hu aapko,

Badal jaaye agar maali, chaman hota nahi khali

Baharein phir bhi aati hain, bahare phir bhi aayengi

My daughter asked me a very tricky question the other day, "Papa, how many breakups have you experienced in your life?" She knows I am a public figure and would have experienced many kinds of breakups. I said, "Don't ask me. At this age, it is very embarrassing to tell your kids about a breakup or failure. However I did say many. If I write a book someday which I do feel like, I'll write a book called 'The last breakup'." Do you know why? This novel is just because the person who was waiting for me necessitated these breakups. The person who was destined to come in my life, for that person

I had to go through all these frustrations, all these breakups. The person who was waiting for me or I can say the person for whom I was waiting. This was from the point of view of my life partner, but sometimes it seems it is not important. If somebody asks me about the secret of my success, I'll take another point of view then. I'll tell them those people who left me in my bad times, I would convey my gratitude to them. Because if they hadn't left me, I wouldn't have met you, Dodani sir, and this platform. At this stage, Sadaf Ji, whether it's the emotional breakup or a business breakup, you know I can tell you with complete authority I never left anyone, people have left me. But breakups are important, they give you and your life depth. You have to handle yourself because somewhere there is someone who is there waiting for you. That's why I moved forward in my life and my life became excellent.

Sadaf Khan: So, this is the reason you got such a wonderful person in your life because obviously when you go through so many things in your life then only the best thing or person will be there for you.

Jawahar Dodani: This is from my personal experience and this is for everybody who is going through some tough times through relationships. I think we tend to realize this at an early stage if it is going to work or not between two partners in a relationship. But for whatever reason, might be kids or society, we keep going and going, like I did for 34 years. I realised and told everybody that you cannot clap with one hand. It was not her fault or mine. She didn't get a husband of her choice and I didn't get a wife of my choice. We both were unhappy. If I could have taken this decision at an early stage like in the first 3-4 years of marriage, even if kids were born, maybe she would have been happy and successful in different ways. I am not saying that we would have remarried or anything but we spent 34 years with each other and we had difficult times. But if we would have taken a quicker decision to separate at that time, then things would have been different. I recommend to everyone whenever I attend any marriage, I give a two-minute lecture to both the partners, that the most important person in your life is your spouse. Other things like money, parents, and kids are not that big in front of your spouse. If it doesn't go well between you two, try for one year at most. Try with all your love, go on therapy or any method you can take but only for one year. After that, if you feel this is not going to work, please move on with your life. If you are young, whether you will marry again or not doesn't matter but you will at least focus on your life differently. Otherwise, the only focus in your life will be how to build a life and how to save all the relationships.

Right now we are building a relationship with each other as Sadaf you are building a relationship with me like a father, with Rajesh sir like a friend. So, a new relationship is evolving because our mind is open and free now. So I would recommend everyone who is listening if you are going to marry again, or even in the case of boyfriend- girlfriend, if it doesn't work between you for one year, please move on. There is a better life out there waiting for you.

Question 5

Sadaf Khan: Sir, The next question is - Many times, we only consider love related to our partner. But maybe in your lives someone is there, not necessarily our partner, but our friend or mother who means a lot and is important. Like I know what Joe Sir's mother means. Personally for me my friends are very important as I can feel the vibe and connection with them. So, is it right that whenever the word 'love' is used, you only think about your spouse or partner or can it be a wider term as well? Can't a soul partner be anyone, either your friend or even your brother? Joe sir, in this regard what do you want to add?

Jawahar Dodani: You know this is

interesting. I say this because after a spouse, there is an inner circle like parents of both partners and kids. I think love is very important in the inner circle because if you cannot respect each other's parents then is there any love between each other? You will love your kids as they are your own but what about each other's parents. I have four sisters, but I say that I have four mothers. My mother has left me with four mothers. They all are younger to me and all love me very much and I love them too. But I feel you are right, you have to have a friend as you cannot share everything with sisters or kids. You know you can open up, talk about everything, fight or get angry as well with your friend. The anger is temporary but to be able to have that is a gift.

In the case of kids, we should let them be like birds, we should let them free when the time comes. But they should know that their mother and father are there. Anytime you want to come back to them, they will always be available for you. If I talk about love, I love

Rajesh Ji, it's a different kind of love, and I have never seen him and never met him. I love you Sadaf as my daughter, it's different. Love is respect, again I'll come back to the point that respecting, caring, and giving is love.

Sadaf Khan: Yes Sir, Rajesh Sir, do you want to add something?

Rajesh Aggarwal: Can you repeat the question, Sadaf?

Sadaf Khan: The thing that I want to know is that whenever we say love, people only think about their partners as in husband-wife or boyfriend-girlfriend, but in this case, can a soulmate be anyone, maybe siblings, parents, or even friends. I want to know your views in this regard.

Rajesh Aggarwal: Dodani Ji has used a beautiful word, inner circle. And I have been thinking about it for the last 5-6 years about who is there in my inner circle. This inner circle, somebody has defined it very well that the people who are there in the inner circle are the people who know everything about you but still they don't judge you, they love you. It is a kind of transparent relationship. For instance, I know everything about Sadaf, Dodani Sir, and Dodani Sir knows everything about me but still I know they will not judge me and accept and embrace me the way I am. So, apart from my life partner, there are a few people in my inner circle. I say with full authority and confidence that you both have been added to my inner circle. I am so grateful to god that I can share everything in life without any hesitation with my inner circle.

Jawahar Dodani: Thank You

Sadaf Khan: This was beautiful. This is what love is all about. I only saw you in the videos. Jawahar Sir might not have known this when I joined you. I have a habit of looking up to people on Google. So I searched and found Joe Sir's picture. I didn't see Jawahar Sir at that time. I guess one week later, we got on a video call. But when we first talked I knew that there was some spark, there was some vibe. In my life, the vibe is very important. I can connect with anyone who I think is going to be pure from heart, I am not talking about materialistic things. And that connection, I felt with Jawahar sir. He brought a change in my life in the last five years. Then I met you, the person whom I saw in videos, and used those videos in my lectures as well. Video with him is a big thing to me. This is growth and love. I feel lucky to be in this video because this is not only about my skills but also the respect and love.

Question 6

Sadaf Khan: What is the basic idea of love, you want people to believe in the generations to come. As things are changing a lot due to digitalization, so are people's mindsets concerning status and money. How important will it be to keep that love alive?

Jawahar Dodani: You know our session may go 5-10 minutes longer because I am going to take a longer time for this question and then Rajesh sir and you both can end it. First, I would start with the question: Who should we love the most and why? For this, I will show you a video. The person you should love the most is yourself. You can say that this is being selfish. When you can't love yourself then how can you love others? You cannot give love to anybody else if you cannot love yourself. Whenever my father feels down even at this age, in his 80s, I bring up this thing, "Dad, go in front of the mirror and remember the good things that you have done" and I know he is not going to do this thing so I list some 5-6 other things for him. Every time he starts loving himself he feels good. We must love ourselves. If you love yourself, you can give love, respect, and care to others. I will show you a video that I watched yesterday. It is about a famous doctor, I think he is from South India. You must watch it till the end, listen to the things he tells. He says that you can even remove your disease with love, that is the amazing power of love.

{Plays a video of a famous doctor, Dr. BM Hegde}

Sadaf Khan: Wow sir! This was very beautiful. I think Jawahar Sir will add something to this.

Jawahar Dodani: You know, I want to add a couple of things. One is that you must love yourself first and when you give love you will get it back. A person who doesn't love himself, will never be able to give love. If you listen to him, you will realise that the healthy mind is the one where if you love people as well as yourself then your mind. And if you do so, your mind will be healthy.

I want to give my example, I do not normally go to doctors except for one or two incidents. I am 66 years old, I have diabetes and I have never exercised. I care for my diet, but it's not that I eat healthy food. Recently, there was an incident and I became unconscious, so I got my brain checked. At that time, they checked every organ in my body, even my teeth. In fact the doctor said that I have the teeth of a 21-year-old. So I feel the person in the video was talking about me, as though I have gone through tough times in my life - financially or due to relationship, I have never let it affect me.

I want to give a gift to you both and the audience. This will be the best gift you ever got in your life. So we let each and everyone bother us in our life. Generally speaking, other people's thoughts and our relationship with them tend to overwhelm or astonish us. So today I want to give you a lock and a key. I have a lock right here (pointing at the brain) and I have its key in my pocket, nobody can enter my brain. Now, to open this lock, they have to get these keys, and right now most people cannot get to my pocket for the key. They cannot find the key and when they try to enter it (head), the lock rejects them. But there are going to be some people in your life, maybe some close friends or family members who will know the whereabouts of the key. Sometimes these close associates steal the key, then they open and get into your head. It will bother you if somebody gets into your head, but it will depend on you as to how much you clean up and get them out of your head. Before sleeping, I clean up my mind and change my lock and key. This way that person will not be able to get into my head. Occasionally some of the things remain there. If a person gets each and everything out of the head, then that will be the best thing. Your health, money, and relationship depend on love. Now, I would like Rajesh sir to close this session.

Rajesh Aggarwal: Sadaf, I think after Dodani sir summarized everything beautifully, there is nothing left to add on more. However, I would like to draw attention to a phrase by the Doctor in the video. He is pretty famous in Hyderabad and deals in wellness. I have been listening to his speeches and want to thank Dodani sir for bringing in his video today. So he says that if you are talking from an I point of view, it is an illness and if you are talking from a V point of view, it is wellness.

Also Sadaf you had asked, how the coming generation should carry love. Frankly speaking, I am very confident in this current generation because I have seen a major shift in their sensitivity. Not only are they sensitive but alert as well as loving and caring. So, I have hope in them. Maybe it's my perspective or maybe I have met only such kind of people from the current generation. Whatever it is, I want to lead this with great hope for this generation. In this Corona pandemic period, the young generation worked for their parents and relatives by quickly arranging medicine and money from donations. So Sadaf I am happy to see these young kids and their method of working. I think we should all learn from this generation instead of teaching them.

Sadaf Khan: Yes sir, with this hope I can only say Love is all you need. To summarize this session, I would say Khuda hi mohabbat hai aur mohabbat hi khuda hai. I am very happy and thankful to both our esteemed guests, Jawahar sir, and Rajesh Sir. Your views are going to help in the betterment of life of the people. As I have already said, this talk is raw and real because you don't need to strive to be perfect, you just need to work on the reality and you need to be real. With this, thank you everyone for joining. We will be back with another episode.

Jawahar Dodani: If you like this episode, please pass it on to your friends, kids, family, parents. Let's end on this note but never say goodbye as we will be back soon!

❑

Session 3

Shades of Money: Good-Bad-Ugly

Sadaf Khan: Hello Everyone! Welcome back. I am your host, Sadaf Khan.

So today's session is going to be very good because we are going to talk about the most interesting as well as the most controversial topic that is MONEY. How important is money? Is money everything or is it just important for work?

So in today's session, we have a very special guest with us Mr. Jawahar Sushila Bhagwandas Dodani. I am pretty sure that till now you all already know a lot about him. He is the founder of LoveZero, uplift1mom.org and many other entrepreneurial ventures. Born and raised in Ahmedabad, he is now settled in America since the last 39 years. He is also a Real Estate broker dealing in lands with this and is constantly working for the upliftment of human life. He has also been awarded the title of "Land Guru" in the US.

Along with him, we have our next guest from India, Mr. Rajesh Aggarwal. He is also known as a thought transformer and you should definitely see his videos on youtube if you haven't till now. Mr. Rajesh Aggarwal. A person who can transform the thoughts of any person he meets through his unique approach of questions and logical deduction. He is someone who questions the old mindset and creates a new mind frame, something he has been doing for the last 27 years.

So let's start our session with a warm welcome of Jawahar sir and Rajesh sir.

Hello sir, welcome to our third episode of Heart To Heart Conversation, and today's topic is money. I am curious and excited about this interesting session.

Jawahar Dodani: Thank you so much Sadaf.

Rajesh Aggarwal: Thank you!

Question 1

Sadaf Khan: So let's start with the most basic and simple question that people generally ask: How much is money important to you?

Jawahar Dodani: You know Sadaf, I would like to answer this question differently.

You should go and ask a homeless person about the importance of money. Go and ask small shopkeepers how much money is important, ask any hawker in the street this question, ask any engineer, doctor, or successful business person that how much money is important? Ask this question to the world's richest people like Ambani or Ratan Tata sir or Bill Gates. And every time you will get a different answer. For some of them 500 rupees is a lot of money and some will not be okay with 5 lakhs or 5 crores.

So about this question, how much money is important, ultimately the answer is an individual's personal perspective. Like whatever money a homeless person can get is enough because he can get bread. But to some it might be less as homeless people do not have a house and everyone needs a roof on their head. People also need good clothes and a car. Some might also say that it is not necessary to have a car, you can use a scooter. While some might say why have a scooter when you can use cycle. As to the need of clothes, you can get a pair of clothes for 100 bucks or even in lacs, you can even get donated clothes. If we talk about food, then one might think where does a Jain or Buddhist monk bring food from? What do they have? So it is also about how much importance you pay to what. Recently, Ambani's right-hand man, who used to earn millions and had a huge property became a monk. I hope you are getting my answer.

Sadaf Khan: The way you explained is great. I know people will connect to this. Rajesh sir, I would like to ask you the same question: How important is money?

Rajesh Aggarwal: Hmmm Sadaf, I will come to your question but before that I want to share something that I have been thinking about since the last couple of days. As the series is progressing, we are coming in deep alignment and sync with each other. I believe that if 3-4 people of similar mindsets meet then a miracle is nearby. The way this talk is going on, especially what Dodani Ji said, you can say that even my words are similar with just a few modifications.

One of my relatives asked me, "Rajesh Sir, how much money do you earn?" This is a very personal question that nobody should ask anyone. I smiled and replied, "The God who is above gives as much as is needed." And that is what Dodani Sir has also said. I reached a point during my training when I got to know that the teacher of my teacher used to earn that much in a year that is needed by him. He used to say if he can't live his life then what is the need for money. So, there are three categories of money, one is needed, the other is desire and the last is greed. Need means I want a shirt, the one I am wearing is my need. Desire means I want 2-4 colorful shirts because there are various Zoom seminars, so I can use them there. Greed means I want many shirts from the whole world. In short, up to need and desire it is good, but when you go beyond that, towards greed, it causes a great problem for you. I would say if we can create a balance between need and desire, then that much amount of money is enough. This is my version.

Sadaf Khan: There was another question similar to this. First I asked about the importance of money. Money is important, if our stomach is not full then how can we live and survive? But, sometimes like you talked about greed and Jawahar Sir said there are different requirements for different people. So, what is the limit to be set for money that will not let you become greedy? Joe sir, again I am coming to you because I think you will surely want to add something to this.

Jawahar Dodani: You know I have a book on greed on my mind. I have told Rajesh Sir too that I want you to convert it into a book. In my real estate business during 2005, I earned 100,000 dollars every month for two years continuously. Before that, in my 25 years, I never earned 100,000 dollars even in a year. I seriously had a goal that if I earned half a million dollars then I would retire. I earned million dollars for two years but I couldn't retire, why?

There are three words that I don't think I had in the past, have them in the present or will have in the future. I hate these three words. You asked what greed is, and the first word from those three words is greed. I will explain to you in detail. I said I hate these three words but during those two years, those three words entered inside me without my authority or permission. I didn't get to know. I found out about it only when it was late.

When greed comes into our minds, we start to gamble, which is the second word. Gamble is not only about casinos and all but it is about expanding the business. I have 1 million, I want to make it 100 million, if we have 100 million then how can we make it 1000 million then 10000 million and so on. We gamble and take risks without even thinking about it. Why gambling comes with greed. Why do those three words that I hate the most get inside my head? I feel that our minds become stupid. Due to greed and then gamble, we tend to lose our minds. Thus the third word is Stupid.

I will tell you a humorous story associated with these three words. So Greed starts with G, gambling starts with G and stupidity starts with S. I thought I should write a book on this and give examples. I will take myself as the first live example and tell about the things that I suffered later on. I was sitting with my friends and sharing all of this. I said I want the third world to start with G but it should mean stupidity. I didn't get any words in the English language. Greed, gambling, and what else. There was another Gujarati person sitting with me, you know what he said. He said Greed, Gambling, and Gadheda. Gadheda is a Gujarati word meaning Donkey and representing stupidity. We have a saying which asks why to do things like donkey, meaning stupidly. However, I don't want to categorise the donkey as he is a very hardworking animal. So these are the three words. We will talk about it at a later time.

In conclusion, greed stops us from becoming a great person. When money comes, it brings power which makes one greedy and that in turn puts you down. So, this is how I define greed.

Sadaf Khan: This was wonderful. We all know that there is no end to greed. Rajesh sir, I would ask the same thing, if there is any amount fixed that will be enough for me to be happy and satisfied.

Rajesh Aggarwal: See Sadaf, I will say it depends on individual mindset. I am just rephrasing Dodani Sir's words.

One mindset is: Sai itna dijiye, Jisme kutumb samaye, Main bhi bhuka na rahun, Sadhu na bhuka jaye.

Another mindset is how Henry Ford described when someone asked him about how much money should be earned. He replied jokingly, earn money as much as your wife can spend (laughing).

The third is, people like Tata, Narayan

Murthy sir, Warren Buffett, all earn money. But if you look closely they do not work for money. There are two phases, one is we work for need and the other is we work for joy. When we work for joy, money doesn't hold an important place but passion becomes important.

So, my perspective is, there should be a phase in life where you do not work for money but a passion. Money will come but it will be used in philanthropy and big things like you have seen Dodani Sir, his dream, and vision about Dodani world. If I talk about myself, then I have told Dodani Sir that after 2025, I will not work for money. I will need money but I don't want myself to think about it, let it be an auto flow. I want to contribute to people's lives. So, this depends on an individual but somewhere or the other I think there should be that one stage where we should be free from money and start working towards changing people's lives. This is a bit philosophical, I don't know if it is an exact answer or not but I am not getting anything more than that in my heart.

Sadaf Khan: Sir, it is philosophical but it is very important and a reality of living a good life that after a time, you need to help others. My thinking is this: Even if you are earning 100 rupees, and you can help with 2 rupees only, then also you should go ahead with it.

Rajesh Aggarwal: I wanted to ask you Sadaf, we both have given our version but your final touch about it is also very important.

Sadaf Khan: I shared a small incident with Joe sir earlier. When I was doing my MBA, we used to get a small pocket money other than the regular hostel expenditure. We decided to start a small voluntary organization where you could donate 10 or 50 or 100 rupees, as per your desire. There were some girls from the hostel and some other friends who donated. At that time, I will not say we did something big, but yes we provided stationery to needy kids. We gave around 4 pencils and one notebook for 10 kids and the smile on their faces was precious. I feel if we think, then we will keep thinking, but what we should do is start at that moment only. I wake up in the morning and the first person who asks me for help, I give him something. This is my personal opinion.

Rajesh Aggarwal: Very beautiful. It is a very deep thought that you shared.

Question 2

Sadaf Khan: The next question is based on today's life. We talk about balancing. Sometimes or the other we see that we lose our self-respect or we lose our personal life due to money. Is that right? When it comes to such a situation, we earn good money but we end up thinking about money every time, even while sleeping and waking. It also affects our relationships at some point. I would like Rajesh sir to give his views on this first.

Rajesh Aggarwal: This is my favourite topic and question that you asked.

I always say this in my sessions that keep balancing between urgent and important. Urgent can be a tender, a contract, or a negotiation and it will give you enough money. Important is when you are going outside and your daughter asks you to buy a bar of chocolate. Don't neglect that chocolate, that's important.

Second is people live life according to the calendar. I will celebrate on 31st December and I will be depressed on 1st January. I don't think this should be life. I think every day can be 1st January. Why can't it be possible? I saw Dodani Sir's display picture in which he is playing in an orchestra, you know he is playing Jazz and he is wearing an amazing dress. That is what life is all about, that you steal a moment out of all the moments. In which you can fulfil your hobbies or sing a song on karaoke or bring your heart into a new mood.

There was a research conducted at Harvard University, where everyone who was 90+ in age was asked if they get their life again, what would they want to do. Maximum people said they want to steal some moments for themselves that they couldn't do. So, this was my version about how to balance things while earning money.

Sadaf Khan: This is beautiful. Now I think Joe sir, your views will help our viewers and friends who joined us today.

Jawahar Dodani: I would like to expand my last answer upon balancing life. Greed, gambling. Why can't you balance your life? I will share my personal experience. Suppose, we have 1 lac rupees, and our income is more than expenses. We have a house, car and children are studying in a good school. Everything is going great. But we want to make 10 lac out of the 1 lac or we have 1 crore and we want to make 10 crores. What happens then? Now, this is the true story of my life during 2005-06. I could have retired but the greed got stuck in my mind, the greed that I didn't know about. I started to gamble without knowing it. And that's what created the imbalance. If I had moved from 1 million to 10 million, it would have been good. Everyone should do this, everyone should try it. When you go from one place to another, it is not wrong but what we tend to do is that we risk that 1 million to make 10 million. We risk our balance because it is not going to increase itself. We risk time and money both. What will be the consequences if you move 1 million to 10 million, the house will become bigger, the number of cars will increase, and will buy new houses, right! But life was good at 1 million also, there wasn't any problem, everything was smooth. It will be a bit good with 10 million but if it goes from 1 million to 0 then what? That is what happened to me, and that situation baffled me just like it would everyone.

The increase in money can cause no difference but the decrease creates problems in balance. That is why when we run behind money, we do not see that we are satisfied with what we have at present. We just keep needing more and taking bigger and more dangerous risks.

If you move forward, nothing will happen but if you move downward it will create problems. That is why I say greed about money is a bad thing but we should try to move up and prevent ourselves from going down.

Sadaf Khan: Sir, this was wonderful. If you cannot enjoy your present, then it is very difficult to imagine happiness in our future because this becomes a habit. It is our present that shapes our future.

Question 3

Sadaf Khan: Some people say money can't buy happiness and some people say money can buy happiness. What are your views on this? It is very simple but is it not necessary to consider a lot of money? Is it true that money can't buy happiness? I think this is a very interesting question on which we can discuss a bit.

Jawahar Dodani: You know whether money buys happiness or not. Of course, if you ask people then 99% of them will say that money brings a lot of temporary happiness. But when does it bring happiness? First, our needs get fulfilled, one should get happiness in this too but we need more because we think we will get more happiness. If we get a bungalow and car, then our happiness will increase, right? Of course, it will increase and we will get happiness. If there is someone who says he doesn't get happiness with money then he or she is lying. Money is such a thing that you can do a lot of things with money in hand. I bought this jacket with money. I couldn't get this jacket if I had no money. So, we can get a lot of things with money. I am sitting in this house otherwise I wouldn't be here. Yes, we get happiness but after a certain amount what is money?

I will give an example. When I said I had a limit of half a million then it increased to million then billion and so on, after a certain time money became just another material object. It will give you superficial happiness. If you want to know if money can make you happy then read the last letter of Steve Jobs, Founder of Apple Company, when he passed away in his fifties. There are various successful people, listening or reading their thoughts in the last moments when they passed away: 'What we spend our time on, wished we would have spent time differently.' And everyone gets happiness from different places. Money will bring happiness up to a certain point or limit, beyond that it brings power, not happiness. In one way you can get happiness with power too, I am not going to deny that. I want to present that video where someone reads the letter of Steve Jobs. It is very much important to know what the person who was a billionaire has to share. There are many more examples like this.

Sadaf Khan: So sir, basically you want to say that after a certain point, money can bring happiness but it depends on people differently. Now without wasting any time, let's listen to Rajesh sir, what he has to share on this?

Rajesh Aggarwal: Dodani Sir ended his view on a very great point. He gave me this opportunity to add to it. It depends on the definition of happiness. Right! If its definition is based on external materialistic things which can be bought with the help of money, then money can bring happiness. If the definition is based on happiness from within which cannot be bought with money, then money cannot bring happiness. So, first, we need to define happiness from a person's perspective. If he or she wants to buy a vehicle, house, clear loan, settle down financially, etc. then it is a different thing. As Abraham Maslow discussed in his theory of hierarchy of needs, the first need is survival, the second is emotional, next is financial, then self-realization. The journey ends there and the inner journey begins.

So, this is a subject of some discussion. I remember once Swami Vivekanand, India's one of the biggest spiritual masters, went to London or maybe he was in India during the rule of the British. One of his teachers asked him, what would you choose if there is money on one side and wisdom on the other side? A person like Swami Vivekanand said he will pick up money, he already has a lot of wisdom (laughing) because at that time he needed money. The financial condition was very bad in his family. So, it depends on the definition of happiness. If it is about the outer world then you need money, if it is about the inner world then money cannot do anything in it.

Sadaf Khan: Yes sir, there is a thin line between happiness and peace. The thing I believe is that money can bring you happiness but it cannot give you peace. You will be happy for some time but the difficulties in your mind will stay there that won't allow you to be at peace.

Question 4

Sadaf Khan: Now I have one very important question and everyone is going to have different views to this question. As this session is heart to heart conversations, let's see what different views we can get.

The question is: what is that one thing which you cannot give up for money? Some people are very ambitious, they work day and night. Their work is everything for them even if they do not gain respect, they continue working as long as they are getting paid. Maybe they are content with it. On the other hand, some people are happy with their 9 to 5 job. Beyond that they do not wish to give up their me-time to anyone or any company or organization for more growth. So, I want to know your opinion on this.

Jawahar Dodani: I will give an example. Around 40 years ago, I was in Ahmedabad and I had a friend Mashib Majumdar, his wife's sister and husband were both professors in a Science college. There were a lot of tuition centers at that time and they could make a lot more money in tuition than salaries. Once we were sitting in a backyard and I was around 25-26 years at that time. I asked them this question, they told me they do not do tuition. Both of them gave the same answer when I asked: Why don't you take tuition classes, you are young and you will earn a lot of money in less time? You know what they said, I remember it till now, they said, "Joe, we have two kids (5 or 8-9 years maybe). If we come back and we both are tired of tuition and household work then we will just go to sleep. But we cannot spend time with our children. Now, at present when we go to bed, I talk to my kids about the moon, stars and tell them stories. How will I be able to do these things in that scenario?" At that time I didn't have kids, I wasn't even married. I didn't have any idea about what he was talking about but now I realize what he said was correct. I spent time with my kids but I don't think I was like them. When I came to the US, I was struggling and many things were going on. Also, I am a bit workaholic, maybe I had a bit of greed for money too. Even though I heard them, I don't think I applied them to my life. Sorry, can you repeat your question?

Sadaf Khan: What is the thing you cannot give away for money?

Jawahar Dodani: So, the answer they gave was amazing. They also needed money, they were not very rich. They were professors, not business people, so they were average people. They would have been taking tuition now, I don't know what they are doing now. But what they did for their children, the money they sacrificed for them was for their happiness which lies with spending time with their kids rather than earning money. What do we do with the money? We get happiness, like when we buy a big house we get happiness. Just a few moments ago, Rajesh Sir shared that what makes you happy is more important.

Sadaf Khan: Sir, this is beautiful. Rajesh sir, I want to ask the same question from you. What is that thing for money which you will not give up?

Rajesh Aggarwal: You know Sadaf, I said in the beginning that whatever I will say, I will say from my experience. When you asked the question I was thinking about whether to give a bookish answer or to give an answer based on experiences I have gained from my life because that will be a more genuine answer.

So, there are two things in my life. See, my training career has been for about 28 years. I started in '93 and I am the oldest in this training after Shiv Khera Sir. So, when I was at my peak as a speaker, now I am in the coaching line, I got project offers from those companies that I don't usually work with. For example, I do not smoke, I do not take tobacco products. The point is I got offers from those companies who wanted me to train their teams that were a smoke or tobacco Product Company. I told them that even if you give me millions of money, I will not sign this contract with you because of the things that I do not consume myself, how can I promote them to others? The things that my soul won't allow me to do, I can't take them up. I got various opportunities at that time but I refused to do those things that my heart did not allow and that was the first thing that I gave up. I used to charge 3 lac rupees for a day at that time and it was a lot of money too.

Secondly, my daughter studied in a boarding school and they organized a meet every 2 months in which the presence of parents was mandatory. So, during that time I refused to do any program regardless of any huge amount of money. Just now Dodani Sir talked about this. I was thinking about the things that I left for money, I remembered Salman Khan's father Salim Khan once said, "If you want to know a person then there are some friends who are their identity." I am lucky that I have a friend who has been with me since class 6, he doesn't even know who I am, and he doesn't know who Rajesh Aggarwal is. Whenever I meet him, he asks me if I am getting my four square meal or not. I never told him about my job, and I don't even want to tell him about it because I want to spend that precious little moment with him when he gives me kulhad wali chai (tea in an earthen cup) by sitting next to me. I don't want my profile to come in front of me. So, these are the things which I won't give up for money. God will give me money but I will not ever leave these little moments.

Sadaf Khan: These are such wonderful and amazing experiences. When we started this session, I said that we will not keep it perfect but we will definitely keep it raw and real. So the things that are coming out now, I think that the experience of you both, the eminent personalities that are joining with us will teach a lot of things to the people of my age and the upcoming generation.

Question 5

Sadaf Khan: The last question and the most important question for this session. What are the suggestions or we can say friendly advice you would like to give to future generations or the viewers who watch us about how to deal with money? How much importance should be given to it? You can share your short view on this. I think I can learn many things from you in the time I spend while conducting this session and discussing different things.

Jawahar Dodani: Rajesh ji, you go first. I want to end this, I want to discuss something important.

Rajesh Aggarwal: I wanted to say the

same that let me start first and then you can conclude.

You know Sadaf there is a quotation by John Powell, who was a great speaker and orator in the US, as well as the father of a church. The quotation goes like, "It's a law of human life as certain as gravity, to live fully one must learn to use things and love people not love things and use people." I have never read any better quotation than this. He compared the law of gravitation to the law of human life. So, I would like to tell the upcoming generation to keep money at its place and keep people at their place, do not ever replace them. Keep currency like a currency and use it as much as you want, but love people. Now, I would like Dodani Sir to conclude.

Jawahar Dodani: You know Rajesh Sir, You quoted the lines of John Powell and said to not use people rather than things, but love people and use things. How to do it? I will answer this. Because there is a huge difference between saying something and actually doing it. 'Do not use people for things but use things to get people' I liked this quote also a lot, I never heard of it before.

The only way you can do this is if you can respect and enjoy money but not fall in love with money. I will tell you how? When you respect and enjoy money, then you will never use people for your gain. But the day you start loving money, you will definitely start using people, this is my personal experience. Whenever you start loving something, you want more and more. The only way to do it is by using other people. So, you have to respect and enjoy the money. There is Goddess Lakshmi in our Hindu religion, people say don't make her angry. If you make her angry, you will not get money. Worship Goddess Lakshmi and what Lakshmi Ji says is to love humans, more than money. If you are a pure soul and kind to people then the goddess will stay with you. That is what Lakshmi Ji says, rather than just worshipping her. People nowadays worship God and Goddess and go around using other people, that is why God does not help them.

The thing that I wanted to say in the end is to love people and respect money but do not use people. People talk about unethical things, like cheating others for money as money has a higher place in their life. Money is good to a certain point and also it brings you happiness. But if you start loving money then with this comes power and this power is a dangerous thing. There are other ways to gain power, like by being politically active, religious, being a celebrity, etc. but if you use them in the wrong way then that is incorrect. Moreover, when you get power through money, then the people who get this do not care or think about others. They don't care about anything else but money in their account. This is called love with money and the power that comes with it. So, please enjoy and respect the money, make lots of money but do not bring power with money. If you don't bring power or I would say ego then Lakshmi Ji will stay with you for a longer time. Thank you.

❑

Session 4

Worldly Buddha: Live Like a Buddha without Being a Monk

Introduction

Sadaf Khan: Hello everyone, welcome to our 4th session of "HEART TO HEART CONVERSATIONS". This session is going on spiritual aspects of our life.

We again have two special guests that are constantly guiding and sharing with all of us. I am sure everyone knows them by now as you are listening and watching them. But for the sake of first time joiners, I will re-introduce them once more.

Allow me to introduce to you all Mr. Jawahar Sushila Bhagwandas Doodani. He is the founder of LoveZero, uplift1mom.org and many other entrepreneurial ventures. Born and raised in Ahmedabad, he is now settled in America since the last 39 years. He is also a Real Estate broker dealing in lands with this and is constantly working for the upliftment of human life.

Now for the second guest of the show, also known as thought transformer - Mr. Rajesh Aggarwal. A person who can transform the thoughts of any person he meets through his unique approach of questions and logical deduction. He is someone who questions the old mindset and creates a new mind frame, something he has been doing for the last 27 years.

Welcome Joe sir, welcome Rajesh Sir.

Today's topic is Worldly Buddha: How to make our lives better?

Question 1

Sadaf Khan: As you know, nowadays, if we can see that people are troubled. We don't necessarily know the reason, but we never fail to show our troubles to others. So, I will ask you some questions which are relatable to people of all age groups but especially youngsters. As today we are talking about Buddha and his teachings. So, my first question is: what is the concept of Buddhism? I would like to ask Jawahar Sir first, how will you define Buddhism? And how can Budhha's teaching help people?

Jawahar Dodani: Well, I would like to first share with the audience that this communication or conversation has been designed by Rajesh Sir and Sadaf, so I don't know what questions they are going to ask and thus I have not prepared any script. Whatever I say is coming directly from my heart and what I feel about it. So apologies if I sometimes go off topic or add some experience to explain.

So, coming back to the question you are asking about Buddha and Buddhism. I rarely watch TV series, but I liked watching the series about Buddha. In the last one year or 7-8 months when I was at home during the Covid period, I started watching 1-2 episodes of it. It was amazing. I started thinking about Buddhist monks. I always thought if I want to be like Buddha, not to be Buddha but to be like Buddha, should I have to leave these things like family, money, livelihood, and the things I want to do. Do I have to leave everything and be a monk? So, I started studying monks. I thought that it would be difficult and would not be possible for me to leave everything and be a monk.

So I thought of alternative methods. How we don't have to leave everything and can still adopt the teachings of the Buddha in our life? So, I am trying, and I had been trying to adopt his teaching and I will do this in the future too till I am in this wonderful world. Basically, Buddha was a self-contained person. They see the things happening around the world, but it doesn't affect them. They are into themselves; they focus on their vision. Whatever is happening around them in present or past doesn't matter to them. If we can achieve this in ourselves then I think we can start living a little like Buddha. If we face issues and challenges in the world one by one, I think that is the starting of you becoming like the Buddha.

Sadaf Khan: Wonderful answer sir, this is what we believe and that is the motivation to have chosen the topic of the sessions. I would like to ask the same question to Rajesh sir, what is Buddhahood according to you?

Rajesh Aggarwal: First, thank you Sadaf

for being a bridge between the two of us (Rajesh Aggarwal and Jawahar Dodani). Without this bridge, both roads would be worthless. So, thank you very much. And thank you Dodani Sir for giving me this opportunity to put my thoughts about this here.

Now, coming back to Buddhahood. See, before Buddha, there was a thinking that to attain a higher mental stage you have to leave your home and go in search of answers. Buddha also did the same thing, he left his home. But when he returned, he never advised anyone to leave their homes, instead, he said you have to wake up, you don't have to run away. I will repeat, you have to wake up, you don't have to run away. That means you have to find the cosmos between the chaos. You have to show your identity in the crowd. You must show your individual mind instead of copying whatever the crowd is thinking. So, according to me as Dodani Sir has said, I would like to add something that Buddhahood means being in the crowd but you are not a part of that crowd, you walk with the crowd, but you maintain your individuality. That's called Buddhahood.

Sadaf Khan: That was a beautiful answer, whatever we are watching now and for people connected spiritually, they will take lessons about how to live life.

Question 2

Sadaf Khan: Moving forward, I would say that if we talk about the qualities of Buddha then there are thousands of qualities but if you want to take some of his qualities then what will be those? I would like to ask Joe sir, which qualities do you wish to adopt from Buddha?

Jawahar Dodani: This is an amazing question, because my biggest weakness that I have to improve or work upon is my anger. I have also talked to Rajesh Sir and Sadaf about it many times. I get upset and frustrated if someone is unfair. How do I control that? So, there is a story about Buddha that I try to recollect everytime I get angry.

There was a saying among people that you can say anything to Buddha, he will never be angry or upset. A man came from far away and challenged people that he would make the Buddha angry. He went to him and started shouting for 15-20 minutes, he said many bad things about him. Buddha was just smiling all the while listening to him. When the man got tired, he asked Buddha, "I said many bad things about you, and how can you be so calm?" He turned to the man and said. "If you bring a gift for someone and that person did not accept your gift, then whom will the gift belong to? Who will own that particular thing which you brought as a gift?" The man replied, "It would belong to me as the person did not take it and I brought the gift." After hearing this, Buddha said, "In the same way, whatever you said in the last 20-25 minutes, I heard but I did not accept it. I did not accept your anger so it falls back to you, as it belonged to you." The man understood, clasped his both hands, and said, "Now I know why people talk about you and respect you." So, in the same way in this world, we should take all the good things and teachings and we shouldn't accept the things we don't like.

I get angry and frustrated; I feel sad when other people do not respond in the way I want them to. But I have to learn that my reaction or response and thinking are not going to be the same as other people. I want to learn this patience from Buddha and I am trying to do this.

Sadaf Khan: Wonderful answer and story sir. Some people do not know their weaknesses, I think it is difficult for them. When we know our weaknesses and accept them then we try to solve them without blaming others. It is a very big achievement; this is what I believe. Now I would like to ask Rajesh Sir, what qualities do you want to adopt in your life?

Rajesh Aggarwal: Sadaf, it is a big coincidence, the story Dodani Sir told was the same story that was going on in my mind. So,

I would like to give him the credit and I even clapped when he told this story. But anyway, one more thing that I want to add is that whatever I have read, learned, knew, and felt about Buddha, he knew the art of making the best from the worst. He saw potential even when no one saw it.

For example, you must know about the story of the dacoit Angulimal. He had a resolution of wearing a necklace of 1000 fingers by cutting it off from people. He was able to collect 999 fingers and only one was left. At that time Buddha entered his village. His disciples had already warned him not to go to that village as a ruthless dacoit lived there. Buddha told him that he has a rule in his life that he doesn't look back or run away. When Angulimal met Buddha, he said, "You are at the wrong place, you can't imagine what you will have to face." Buddha replied, "I know what I have to face from the time I got to know myself. Whoever you want to kill is already dead, you can't kill. I have one element in me which you can never kill." Angulimal said, "You don't know that I will cut your finger to make a necklace." Hearing this, Buddha replied, "Sure, but I will ask you to do a small thing. Just pluck a flower from anywhere and give it to me. Then you can make your necklace." He plucked a flower and gave it to Buddha. The Buddha then responded and said, "The way you plucked it, now go and restore it to the plant and then you come back and cut my finger." Angulimal replied, "How can we restore it after plucking the flower." Buddha replied, "That's what I wanted to say, you know how to break things and I know how to restore them. The person who cannot restore things is an incomplete man. Come with me, I will teach you to restore."

This story has had a huge impact on my heart. Wherever we go, we should know how to connect everything and everyone. What Dodani Sir is doing in Heart To Heart Conversation is also about connecting people. Not for money, but for love, compassion, and building relationships. So, that is what we are doing, we are following his teachings only. So Sadaf, this is the quality that I like the most.

Sadaf Khan: Beautiful! In today's world, it is very difficult to build relationships, but very easy to break relationships over very small matters. This is a big lesson we are getting today: If a thing breaks then it is very difficult to restore it so it is better to not break anything. It would be easier to not come to that point of breaking. If we accept our mistake, apologize soon then no one will become big or small.

Question 3

Sadaf Khan: There is a thing in our mind that if you want to achieve Buddha state then you must leave your world as Jawahar Sir already talked about it. There are a lot of people living in this confusion. So, I want to ask Jawahar Sir if it is necessary to leave our world and sit on a mountain. Is it that then only we can achieve Buddhahood or is there any other way. Though you talked about it a little bit, still I request you to elaborate so that we get more clarity.

Jawahar Dodani: See, it is very difficult to become a monk because you have to leave all your desires. We, human beings, have a lot of desires like we need partners, kids, friends, house, money, car, food, etc. These are our desires and to leave all that and become a monk is not possible. But if you can leave them, then the life of a monk is very simple. After that, you have to go to an ashram or mountain, you don't have to do any work, you don't need to answer anyone, you just have to meditate and talk to other people. The conclusion is that the process of becoming a monk is very difficult but after becoming one, life gets easier. So it is up to an individual as to what he wants to do.

However, I think it is impossible to be a monk, or I can say it is not impossible, but it is immensely difficult. We are trying to study Buddha humanly and I think the life of an ordinary person is much harder than a monk. If we want to adopt the qualities of Buddha in our own life, then that is much harder. That is what I am trying to do, that is what we are trying to cover in this session.

Sadaf Khan: Yes sir, I think this question always bothers people in some way or the other that to be a better person, you have to leave the world. But it is not necessary.

I want to ask the same question to Rajesh sir, what are your inputs into it?

Rajesh Aggarwal: Can you repeat the question? I want to refresh it.

Sadaf Khan: Sure sir. There is a thing in our mind that if you want to achieve a Buddha state then you must leave your world, you must go away on a mountain or some place, leaving everyone and everything behind. So is it necessary to do this or is there any other way? I don't think anyone will become Buddha but even if we want to be like him a little, is it possible without leaving anything.

Rajesh Aggarwal: Sadaf, the knowledge and realization I have, according to me, Buddha is not a name of a personality but a mental state. Secondly, it is not a destination but a continuous journey. The journey levels up as we proceed. I think that if we start at a small scale, it becomes big. An atom contains a lot of power, a single ray of sun is enough to remove darkness. If we adopt only one technique from Buddha or from all his teachings, that is, if we delay the reaction, then it will not be added negatively in our karma. Buddha gave this law of karma if someone says anything to you and you delay your reaction. If we begin with this, we can move towards Buddhahood. To be Buddha or like Buddha is not in my capacity, but we can adopt a little part of him and that is what I think.

Sadaf Khan: It's great sir. If we can even learn 10% from him, not only at present but in the future too, we will try to make the world like that. The world changes when we change ourselves. If you change yourself, that will be the biggest victory.

Question 4

Sadaf Khan: As it is rightly said, that after a dark night comes a bright morning. Whenever there is sadness, happiness follows, after a storm comes great weather. As we are observing that there is a lot of negativity that is prevailing around us. People do not trust each other and maybe it is because of the things we are going through. So, Rajesh sir, do you think the future belongs to the worldly Buddha? As I think, we people will wake up someday and start acknowledging the importance of relationships and will begin to cherish and become like a Buddha.

Rajesh Aggarwal: Yes, it is a great question Sadaf. From my vision, certainly, the future will belong to the Worldly Buddha. We need to attain peace and real peace is what you attain by being in the world rather than getting it after leaving the world. If I attain peace outside of my surroundings at any other place, then I will lose my peace if I come back to my surroundings. The real fun remains in having a mountain of peace inside me while being in this worldliness. Then only I will move towards the real Buddhahood. The coming future will follow Buddha's concepts, teachings, philosophies, and techniques. What we are doing will act as a catalyst in this process. This is my thought.

Sadaf Khan: You gave an exceptional answer. Joe sir, what are your views on this: about the future belonging to the Worldly Buddha?

Jawahar Dodani: You know my answer will be a little contradictory. I don't know your next questions, though I am answering this now that can be related to other questions. But first I would like to answer how to be Buddha? Buddha was a very rich person, his father was a king. When he was born, it was said that he would either be a great king or a religious leader. So, the king kept him inside the palace to prevent him from seeing any sadness.

He got married and had a kid and once they went to visit a place outside his city's boundary.

He saw the misery of people. At first, he saw an old person and he said that you will become old one day, next he saw an ill person who said that he will also be ill, at last, he saw a dead body being carried away, and the people said you will also die one day. At last he saw a wandering monk that made him curious to find the root of all human suffering so, he became a monk named Buddha to seek answers to these things in life.

But I don't agree with this because he said that he wanted to go away from the miseries of this world. I think those things he saw were not miseries, I am not going against Buddha or anyone, but this is my personal opinion. Those things are events of life. Today, we accept the occurrence of day and night, whenever there is a good or bad event, like marriage, the birth of a child are all events of life, in the same way, a car accident is also an event although it is bad. For me, illness, aging, sickness and death are also events of life and not miseries. The reason is if you think of them as events, you will not be sad. I talk about death every day that I will leave this world someday. Though I do have one wish that I want to know one year in advance that I am going to die. Buddha already knew that he was going to die in a few years . I need at least 6-12 months, I don't know why but I don't want to leave suddenly like my mother. My mother got ill at night and she was gone in 2-3 hours. We neither said goodbye nor did we meet with her.

So, I don't think of it as miseries but rather as events. You talked about the challenges of life and what will be there in the future. You should think of everything as an event, it will eventually pass, so it doesn't matter what that event is. It doesn't matter if that event is good or bad, it will be gone. Politicians change, earthquakes or storms occur, everything comes and goes. I agree it gives us some problems. So, these events sometimes give us happiness and sometimes sadness. Whenever anything happens, face it and find some solutions for it, enjoy it or be sad for some time, but think of it as an event. I try a lot.

This way Peace will come in your life because these events will come and go. At present, this session we are doing will also end in half an hour. We are enjoying ourselves right now, but this is also going to end, and we will go back to our work. So, enjoy the moment, this is the way I look at it.

Sadaf Khan: This is exactly what our session is about heart to heart conversations. Everyone is different from one another and has different thoughts.

Question 5

Sadaf Khan: My next question is: as we are living in this world, so is it necessary that we should be aware of everything? Is it possible to keep complete awareness about everything, be it good or bad? Can we be that level of perfection? Some people might think they are not perfect, as they are not completely aware of their surroundings. This can be related to a relationship, job, or anything? So, sir, is it possible to be aware all the time?

Jawahar Dodani: You know if people are aware of one thing, then there will never be any problem or sadness, and that is whatever action you are doing or saying, is it affecting other people or their lives. If people are aware of this one thing, that they should never hurt others, then I think they will get personal awareness. Many times, we only think if we are affecting other people, animals, or any other life. My mother passed away two years ago, and the way she lived her life for others, not just for her kids was phenomenal. She taught me many things, she is my guru and my god.

But, four weeks ago my son's dog passed away. I don't even like to call him a dog, his name was Dobby, we considered him as a kid. In his last week, he was suffering a lot, and then he was waiting for my son to come home. My son came, he slept with him. He woke him up around 3-4 am in the morning, he cried a little and after 1-2 hours he was gone. I don't know why I brought up this story, but the awareness that my son had, he knew that

Dobby was waiting for him so he left his work to meet him. So, in the same way, we all must be aware of our inner circle, parents, siblings, friends, business associates, etc. We should check if we are hurting them in any way at least intentionally.

Sadaf Khan: Yes sir, the way we want to keep ourselves aware is different and situations are also different. As Rajesh sir gives very important views, so I would like to ask Rajesh Sir, what do you want to add to this?

Rajesh Aggarwal: Dodani Sir has beautifully answered the question especially when he talked about that story. The way I got to know about it today is very touching. We can see the level of awareness in an animal that he knew that the person he loves should come and he wanted to take his last breath in that person's arms only. It is a very great thing and if you ask me if it is possible to be aware of things 24 hours a day, then I will say that it is not possible. I am not like that at least, I won't be knowing everything.

But yes, I am at this level that I delay my reactions. I can delay my negative actions, which I learned from Buddha's teachings. Before doing anything, take a long breath, this breaks the rhythm of the reaction that you were going to show and it helps you to get awareness in the present moment. These are 2-4 things that I follow. For how long I am aware is not important, but if I get this for a very short amount of time, then I think that I am doing something good. This is what I realized till now.

Sadaf Khan: Very nice sir, as Jawahar Sir and Rajesh sir said that it is more important to not hurt other people intentionally. No one can be aware of everything around them, but whatever awareness you have about the surrounding should be utilized in a positive way.

Question 6

Sadaf Khan: Can we balance Buddha state on one side and daily monetary activity on the other side? Is it possible to balance both?

Rajesh Aggarwal: Yes, yes! You can definitely do that. The currency word comes from 'current' which means flow. If you keep money in an Almirah, it will be there like that only, but if you give one rupee to ten different people, its value will increase ten times. What I learned from Buddha is that you don't have to be possessive about anything. The feeling of possessing something makes money bad. Money in itself is not a bad thing, it is a beautiful thing but people destroy it when they become possessive about money, position, and power. So it is possible to balance between monetary growth and the Buddha state. This is something that we need to probably learn that we have to enjoy everything by living in this world, to use everything rather than misusing it. But normally people are unaware and they misuse it. So whatever you said is possible Sadaf.

Sadaf Khan: I agree sir! Whenever you have power and position then the way you use it is very important. Joe sir, as it is our last question, what are your views on this; is this balancing possible? Sometimes monetary activities are important, while other times you want to achieve something humanitarian. So can we manage both?

Jawahar Dodani: You know, you can ask any monk, it is very difficult to be like Buddha but it is easy too. Now you will ask how? I will answer it by telling you about my father's question. My father always asks, "Why are people not humane?" I always have the same answer, "Dad, it is not difficult to be human but having a desire to be human is very difficult." What I mean is, there is no difficulty to be a human, you have to give love and respect, smile more often, help others; it won't cost you anything. It is free. That is being human. That is the main teachings of Buddha, he wanted to love people and himself. He did not want to get angry at what other people say. So, to be Buddha you have to become human first. If you cannot be human, then forget about being Buddha. If you can become human, then you are very close to Buddha. Now, let's compare it with money, family life, and all the things that are happening in the world. It is important to do those things too, you have to earn money, you have to find a partner, house, car, etc. All this will be possible if you become a human first. If you do all these things without being a human first, then you will be far away from Buddha. If you do all these things while being a human, like you need to love, care and help others, then there will be no difficulty to be Buddha.

Sadaf Khan: It is wonderful that if you want to be Buddha then you have to become a human first. It is the basic requirement of life: to be humane. As nowadays, everyone is becoming a robot. Everyone is running away without knowing the destination and reason. So, if we adopt only 10% of the Buddha's teachings, then it will be beneficial to us and those around us. We will transfer positive energy.

As I told everyone in the beginning that this session is going to be spiritual and will give positivity and motivation. I hope all our viewers who watch us, hear us, and like us, have liked this session. With this I will share my tagline, we might not keep it perfect, but we will keep it raw and real. I would like Jawahar Sir and Rajesh sir to speak something to conclude this wonderful session.

Rajesh Aggarwal: First of all I would like to share my gratitude because I got this opportunity to share my internal feelings here at this platform and this is what Buddha has taught, to be in gratitude 24 hours a day. If a person removes criticism and complaints from his or her life then he or she has walked on the path of Buddha. So, I would like to share my gratitude and there is no better feeling than this in me right now. So, thank you that I met you and now I would like to hear from Dodani Sir.

Jawahar Dodani: You know, you all know Rajesh Sir but I feel that I am very fortunate that Rajesh Sir is with us. He is sharing his experience about life with us, he is giving his input and advice to us. And Sadaf! Just wait and watch. In the upcoming 5-10 years Sadaf will become one of the greatest personalities in India. But these sessions that we conduct, when different minds meet, I would devote this to my mother.

As Sadaf said my name in the starting Jawahar Sushila Bhagwandas Doodani, I think I am the first person who put my mother's name in his middle name. I am already transferring my name legally because my mother was and will be everything to me. If there is no mother in this world, then there will be no one, not even Buddha. I think mother is bigger than Buddha. So, respect and love your mother. If you cannot love your mother then forget about doing anything in this world. To end this, I would like Sadaf to tell us about Meri Maayi.

Sadaf Khan: So friends, we are launching our new website, it is a platform called Meri Maayi. It is dedicated to mothers. We will share stories, videos, and quotes that we will put there to dedicate to our mothers. The special thing about this website is that if you have some of your stories related to your mother or if you are influenced by someone like your friend's mother, about their struggle or how they share love in the world, then you can share with us. We will upload them. Our motive is to support mothers who are in need, we will dedicate ourselves to this. As we are doing this session, Joe sir's first video in which he is talking about mothers has been uploaded on the platform. Soon, the website will be finalized in a day or two, then we will launch it. I hope and I think you all will definitely like it.

Thank you, everyone. Thank you Rajesh sir for always being there and always motivating us because we learn a lot from you and your work. So till the wait for our next session gets over, adios.

Jawahar Dodani: Thank you Sadaf, Thank you Rajesh ji.

Rajesh Aggarwal: Thank you.

❑

Session 5

Be World Famous: More than One Way

Sadaf Khan: Welcome everyone, I am Sadaf Khan, your friend and your host for the show "Heart to Heart Conversations". And today's session is going to be the most fascinating and relevant because today we are going to talk about fame and popularity, a common and significant topic for today's generation. Now again we have special guests today, Mr Jawahar Dodani, I would like to take his full name Mr. Jawahar Sushila Bhagwandas Doodani. He was born and brought up in Ahmedabad, India but from the last 39 years he has been in the USA. He is constantly working for humanity. He is the founder of Meri Maayi, uplift1mom, Love zero and Dodani's World. Another special guest we have with us is Mr. Rajesh Aggarwal, many of you know him, you might have watched his motivational videos. He transforms thoughts and he has been working in this field for the last 27 years. Welcome Joe Sir, Rajesh sir and thank you both for rejoining again, people are loving you here.

Jawahar Dodani: Thank you Sadaf, you are amazing. I love talking with you and Rajesh ji. I enjoy these sessions. Sadaf is a young and growing personality and we already know about Rajesh ji. Thank you.

Rajesh Aggarwal: Thank you Sadaf. You(Sadaf) said we both are special but you know we become special when your speciality gets included with us. Thank you

Question 1

Sadaf Khan: So moving on, today's question is: Why is it important to become popular or why is popularity so important nowadays? If we talk about popularity, we can see people are fond of various social media platforms and their features, like Instagram, Instagram reels, Facebook or Facebook stories, etc. People try to use funny content, poetry, or many talents to get popular or famous.

But this is not as easy as it seems, with popularity/fame, one will get loads of questions also and to answer these kinds of questions, we have two special guests with us.

So my very first question is pretty basic: Why is it required to become popular or I can put it differently: is it necessary to become popular? Joe sir, I would love to hear your views on this question.

Jawahar Dodani: You know Sadaf, I don't remember if it was when 5 years, 10 years or 20 years back there was a point in my life where I was crazy about a thought. The thought being "How am I going to become world-famous?" I am 66 years old today.

I wanted to become world-famous, not famous in just my family, neighbourhood, or even my city. I was crazy about this thought and what to do to manifest it in reality. And I always wanted to do good but I also knew that there will be talks or gossip that he is doing just to get fame.

I thought about it a lot but I did not want to hide things or my ambitions. So now if people ask this question to me, I quickly say that yes I do this work to become famous. My craziness is like an open book for everyone. I don't like to hide this craziness. There is also a reason why I want to become famous. It might be my Ego, I don't know. But the real reason behind this thought is something else and I will tell it to you later. I want to become world-famous. I really appreciate you two, Rajesh sir and Sadaf, for helping me with my goal.

So let's move further and see what Rajesh Sir has to say about it.

Sadaf Khan: Rajesh sir, the same question I want to ask of you, Why is it important to become famous in this era?

Rajesh Aggarwal: I don't know about others but since childhood, I also wanted to become famous. I am sharing this for the first time with you all. The kind of environment I was brought up in was not so good. I used general toilets for almost 20 years of my life. The apartment where I was living had only one toilet for the whole apartment. Approx. 20 people were always in a queue to use the toilet. I used to fetch water from a place that was 1-1.5 km far away from my apartment. This was my life. I have lived this life for 20 years straight.

But Sadaf, I used to live near the airport area so I could see airplanes passing over my terrace. It seemed as if I could touch it with my hands.

Right now, no trainer or coach is speaking, this is my inner child sharing childhood memories with you all. I literally used to jump to try to touch the airplane and I always believed that one day I will definitely touch it with my hands. Until the age of 20-25, I had never even seen an airplane from the inside. It was at the age of 27, I sat inside the plane. And trust me, I was feeling that I have achieved something today. I have heard that Sony is a company, whose products sell under 30 seconds or 1 minute all over the world. So I used to think, will such a day come into my life where people will recognize me all over the world. And now with God's grace and support of friends like you and a big brother like Dodani sir, today in every minute someone watches my content or videos on youtube.

So about your question: why is it important to become famous? It is basically food to our soul. For me becoming popular is like food to the soul that gives me energy. And this is the best answer I can give to this question.

Sadaf Khan: sir, your answer was apt and it made me emotional too. I believe when you are connected to the ground, then only can you truly value the sky. I have understood one thing that, if a person is earning 1 lakh rupees, he will value it for sure and be happy. But a person who earns 5,000 rupees and reaches 1 lakh, will value it 100 times more than anyone. For him, that 1 lakh would be more valuable than 1 crore or 10 crores.

Rajesh Aggarwal: I apologize that I am disturbing you in the middle. You have asked us various questions and we talked about some interesting and beautiful topics. But today I want to ask you and know your views on this question. Tell us why is it important to become famous?

Sadaf Khan: Sir, if you ask this question to people you'll probably get the answer that no we don't want fame or we don't like popularity but it is all a lie. Anyhow, what I meant is that everybody wants to get fame or popularity. We all like the thought where everybody knows us through our good work. As you shared about your journey sir, I too have a similar journey. Though, I haven't reached the heights like you, sir.

So as I was saying we share our feelings with others. For example if person A bought a phone of Rs. 15,000 with his hard work and person B owns an iPhone which is far more expensive than the former. But person A has struggled more than person B, he might have had some cheap phones earlier. The phone he owns now will be more valuable in his eyes as compared to the expensive phone person B owns.

In the same way if I get 1000 views on my post, I will be the happiest person and after that the happiness will increase if I get 10 million views. But the satisfaction I got with 1000 views will be more because it was the first time I got so many views. So it basically depends on me. That happiness and satisfaction would be mine, with all the struggle and hard work that I have faced in my journey so far to achieve what I am today. So this is very big, and every person wants to become popular in their own ways.

Question 2

Sadaf Khan: So the second question that I would like to ask is a bit controversial. So, the question is: Is it necessary that you can either be a good person or you can become a famous personality? Is being popular important or just being human important?

Jawahar sir, I would love to hear your thoughts on this.

Jawahar Dodani: You know, like we have discussed in earlier sessions about being a human. So if you are not a good human, can you become popular? Yes, of course, you can. I wanted to discuss that I have researched a lot about how I can become popular. Usually, people don't think about becoming popular while working. But I have a different goal. I want to become popular. I want to get world fame. Great world-famous people might have not thought about becoming world-famous while doing their good or bad work. But clearly, I have a different goal. I have researched on which type of people become world-famous? Why do they become world-famous? So it is not necessary that first, you become a good human and then become popular. No, you can be famous in various ways. But my theory of popularity says that yes, of course, you have to become a good human first then only you can succeed and become popular. And this is the best way to get fame, but this is not a necessity.

Sadaf Khan: Sir, I must say that it was a very clear and precise answer. So Rajesh sir, your thoughts are also important for all of us so please share your point of view.

Rajesh Aggarwal: Sadaf, there is no conflict in saying that if you are popular then you can't be a good human. There is no doubt that a beautiful person or good human comes first over any popularity. But we should know that popularity and good people can always go together. For example, like body and soul working together in the same way, popularity and good humans can go together. We can also compare good humans with the soul and popularity with the body. So a sync between the two can be possible but if I get a choice between the two I would prefer being a good human first and will adopt popularity later.

Sadaf Khan: Yes sir, you have given a very useful answer to this question.

Question 3

Sadaf Khan: Before asking my third question, I want to say something like Rajesh sir had given an example and Jawahar sir, we all know that he is so down to earth and he won't even show how good he is to others. He talks to me with so much kindness and love and similarly he talks to everybody with the same gesture and kind attitude. And this is already a good thing for a person who has achieved so much in life.

So Jawahar sir, my third question is: How can an ordinary human become popular? We all are aware that every person in this world has dreams, everybody wants to move forward and wants to achieve something in their life. And today, social media has helped so many people to get fame or help them achieve something. So sir, how can an ordinary human being become popular?

Jawahar Dodani: Sadaf, this is the topic I have been researching for so many years. And the answer to this question can take 5-10 minutes or more.

Sadaf Khan: Sure sir.

Jawahar Dodani: Who are these popular people in this world and how did they become popular? Let's talk about it. The first group that becomes popular is the one who has wealth, like Ambani, Ratan Tata, Bill Gates, Laurent Baffie, etc. These people have more money than half of America's population. They have money more than India's total population can ever make. So people know these wealthy people by their names. So that is one way you can get popularity.

The second way is Politics. You can see a lot of people in politics. Take Prime Minister Narendra Modi's Example. He started his journey as a Teaseller and now he is The Prime Minister of India. Mr. Obama, the first black person who became The President of the biggest and strongest country in the world, The United States. I am not saying bad or good about anyone or their work. I am just saying how people can make their name in politics. Look at Trump's journey. Most of the people hated him but still, he became The President. That means some people also love him somehow. Similarly, Saddam Hussein is a great example of this. They are all world-famous.

After these two categories, religious leaders come third on the list. If these three options are there for me and I don't have wealth, and no interest in politics, I will end up with the third option which is to become a religious leader. There are a lot of religious leaders in this world who are more popular than everybody, for example, Pope Francis, Guru Nanak Ji, etc. There are a lot of spiritual leaders in India also like Sadhguru and Ramdev Baba. And they all are famous everywhere in this world.

This sounds amazing but can I become a spiritual leader? No, I am just 66 and I have not done anything till now. So this option is also not possible for me. Then the next option is being a celebrity. Now celebrities are of various types. Look at Amitabh Bachhan, who is a legendary actor of Indian Cinema, Cricket legends like Kapil Dev, Virendra Sehwag, TV Star Oprah, and the list goes on. So celebrities are of many types. But these people started their journey from scratch almost 30-40 years ago. People do get lucky and get fame very soon in their life. But can I become a celebrity like them? No, at least not in this life.

My son is trying to become one. He is a 26 years old actor and has done a pretty good job in his field. Maybe until I am alive, my son can become world-famous in acting, production, or directing. He is really working hard towards his goal.

Coming back to the question, I have told you already, that I have researched a lot about it and I have also noted down some points. Then the next thing was invention. Inventions are also of various types. You can see various recent inventions like self-driving cars, billion members on Facebook, Google, Instagram, and so many other things. These inventors have different minds. They do unexpected things and become famous all over the world. Look at Mark Zuckerberg, he started Facebook with 1000$, and see him and Facebook today.

Now the next one is Nobel Prize winners. So the Nobel Prize is a worldwide thing. People do get awarded for their immensely good work like for peace, for scientific discovery, or inventions. But I have no way to become that. Yes, I do admire these people but I can't be one.

Then there is a crime, as you said earlier that it is not important to be good for becoming famous. Every politician does not have to be a good man, not that every wealthy person is a kind man or every spiritual leader is good. Some of them are still in prison for their bad sins. There are a lot of celebrities who have done wrong things in their life, who are not kind to people but still they are famous. So it is not important to be good to get popularity all over the world. Crime can also make people popular, you can see the mafia is a great example. I won't talk much about it. But yes, crime can also be a reason for getting popular. But there is no way I can choose crime to get popular.

So then I was searching how am I going to get popular? Then I saw 3-4 mentors in my life. Like Mother Teresa, but she gave her whole life and then she became popular. Mahatma Gandhi also fought a lot and gave his very crucial years to the people of India, left his family behind, and after that he became famous. Martin Luther King, Nelson Mandela, who fought for their country in every way possible. Then I realized, if I want to become famous, I need to do what I love, I need to do something in which I have an interest in and that is humanity. Humanity is something in which you don't need money, politics, skills or talent, religion, fame, etc. There is no need to do any kind of invention or discovery, no need to be involved in any crime.

So like Mother Teresa, there are a lot of people doing good work for humanity.

For example near Ahmedabad, there is a place (ashram), which was started by a lady. She started with a single room and now that place is so big but she is known only around Ahmedabad or nearby areas. And there are so many people around the world who are still doing this kind of work but not getting fame or popularity. So I wanted to make these people famous worldwide. I want others to know what good work they are doing for humanity. And I thought this is probably the best and only way I can become world-famous. Because I totally don't have that much money, I am not good at politics, I am not a celebrity, don't have any skills like acting, or don't have a great brain like the inventors. So this seemed the last option for me to achieve my goal.

And this is what I am trying my best with the help of you two. And I am hoping for the best to come. So I think I figured it out that this is the way, humanity is the way I can be world-famous. So let's see how everything goes now.

Sadaf Khan: Very nice sir! And the biggest thing is the way you have shared everything in detail is very important and it will be useful to all of us. It is not necessary that you must follow the same path as the other people are going on. You can make your own path like Jawahar sir has done. So thank you so much, sir!

Now Rajesh sir this is definitely incomplete without you. So we want to know your views about it.

Rajesh Aggarwal: You know Sadaf, I was literally lost in Dodani sir's answer that I forgot the question you have asked. The answer was so genuine and beautiful. Then with his series of ways to become famous made me remember the question. So Sadaf I don't think there is a need to disturb this beautiful answer. I just wanted to add only one line to this answer that if we all do good work then popularity and fame will automatically come along with me.

So that's it, I don't think there is any need to add on something.

Sadaf Khan: Thank you so much, sir!

Question 4

Sadaf Khan: Let's move forward to our next question. Many times in our life, when we face difficulty we tend to leave our goal because we think that we cannot follow it due to those difficulties. Jawahar Sir and Rajesh sir as you both have a lot of experience, I think this question will motivate the youngsters. So, the question is how to manage back-to-back setbacks in the journey of becoming popular. In the journey of our dream, there will be difficulties too, how can we manage that? I know Joe sir's views will be very motivating.

Jawahar Dodani: First of all, not many people will like the answer I am going to give. That is, when they cannot move to a greater height, cannot reach the grapes then they say 'grapes are sour.' Right! We don't want to say we cannot reach the grapes. I will give a disclaimer that I want to become world-famous, I have to do this and that and I will try my best but I have decided from day one that whatever I will try if I do not achieve it or do not get enough then I will not be frustrated or sad. I will accept it.

People talk about earning a lot of money but later they say they cannot earn it. One should know that not everyone can earn money. It's okay! I want to become world famous but if I die tonight then what will happen to my dream. That is alright, we have to accept everything. I always say that if you are not happy with what you have today in any area be it health, wealth or relationship then you won't be happy in the future with whatever you will get.

Today you want 1 lac rupees, when you will get it you will want 5 or 10 lac and so on. If you are not happy with 1 lac then you won't be happy even if you get 25 lac or more. The same thing happens in relationships and similarly in my dream of being world-famous. I am famous in my heart and soul. Even if I cannot become famous in the world, people will say Joe has accepted his defeat. Yes, I accept my defeat, yes, those grapes are probably sour for me. But I am what I want to be inside my heart.

Sadaf Khan: Beautiful sir. As I say that for some people 1000 views matter and for some others even 10 lac views do not matter. So, the image you have made about yourself in front of you is all that matters. My mother always says, "When you stand in front of a mirror and become happy with yourself then it is the biggest victory." What I think is whatever audience you have reached, you have reached with a lot of positivity. The people who are listening to us, today is our fifth session, they hear us with a lot of love. This is a big part of your popularity. With this thought, I will move on to Rajesh sir.

If we talk about you then you are in the same field where there are views, social media, and more. There must be a lot of challenges in your way when you upload your videos, there must be some ups and downs in the views. Many people say it doesn't matter but I think it matters a lot. It is a big thing which takes you towards popularity. So sir, what are your views on it?

Rajesh Aggarwal: See Sadaf, I often say this, when I came to Delhi I was 20 years old. My father went bankrupt and we had to move from Calcutta to Delhi in one night. No one knew me in this city and my father died after 6 months. I started my career by selling t-shirts in Palika Bazar. From then till today, if you can see, I have more than 2 lac subscribers and more than 1.5 crore viewers in many countries. Is it not enough for me to be happy? How much more should I ask from God? Isn't it enough to say thank you to God? I agree I do not have 1 or 2 crore subscribers but from where I started, I have got a lot. I will be thankful to God for the rest of my life.

Secondly, I want to say I read a very good

thing yesterday: Some people say that between two nights comes a short day. But other people say that between two days a little night comes. We can say the night is just a small setback that passes. So, if you look from this point of view, tomorrow will be a better day. That is my view.

Sadaf Khan: Lovely sir, the answers you share with us, if I talk about myself it creates positivity from inside which is very important.

Question 5

Sadaf Khan: Now, coming to the next question. Sometimes, when a person becomes famous, he or she moves towards ignorance, a kind of rudeness comes inside him or her toward others. The words 'I' and 'Me' have become so prevalent these days. I would like to quote my mother here again as I learn a lot of things from her. Whenever I share my excitement with my mother about my shoot and everything, it seems that I am flying in the sky and she pulls me back to the ground. She always says, "No matter how high you fly in the sky, don't leave your land." Somewhere it happens that fame takes you towards ignorance. So, Rajesh sir, first I would like to hear your views about this then we will move towards Joe sir.

Rajesh Aggarwal: Please rephrase the question once.

Sadaf Khan: Sir, this fame and popularity sometimes leads to ignorance and rudeness. Is this true? If this is true, then how to deal with it?

Rajesh Aggarwal: Some people say that power corrupts a person, but there was research which says that it does not happen this way, the corrupt person waits for power and when it comes, it unleashes the corruption. For a good person, power and money is just a game, he knows that so he becomes more modest after getting them. So, if a person becomes arrogant and egoistic with power, then somewhere that person had suppressed those feelings inside of him and was looking for an opportunity. This is my view.

Sadaf Khan: I feel it is a very big answer that you gave. I agree that our values are very strong and they will never waver wherever we go, whatever we become. Now, I am very excited to hear Joe sir's answer.

Jawahar Dodani: You know, I have two kids. My daughter is 34 and my son is 27. Both of them are very successful. My daughter is a psychologist, she is helping many young people and adults. My son is an actor, he entertains people. I taught them only one word in life when they were growing that every action has its own consequences. Sometimes these consequences can be seen right away and sometimes it takes a lot of time, maybe 15 to 25 years.

So, my son was interested in politics when he was young and he was doing great. I asked him if he wanted to become the president. I told him, Obama became the president so you can also become the president of America as you are a citizen here and were born here. But, at the age of 18 he did go through a phase of bad behaviour. I don't want to share his bad incidents publicly (laughing). The thing we talk about at present will show its consequences after 20-30 years.

When you run for the Presidency, everyone will bring your history since you were born, your parents' history, what have you done in your childhood, teenage life, and adulthood. I taught them a second word when my kids started getting successful. They were successful at a young age especially in the field of acting, success brings fame. The work my daughter was doing was more important than my son but she was not getting any fame from outside. On the other hand, my son was getting fame from the outside, everyone was talking about him because he did that commercial and the show Atypical on Netflix. Then I realized that I have to share something with him. So I added one more word, being humble. Just now Rajesh ji talked about this.

Always be humble because whether you have success, money, religious power, political power or you are a celebrity, you will definitely get power but this power is good and bad. If you get success in any area and you are humble then what will people say, look at Amitabh Bachhan he is very successful but he is so humble. Ratan Tata is one of the richest men in India and he is very humble. I told my son if you want to be successful, always be humble, otherwise, no one will care or think about you. If you are humble, then people will say good things about you. With power comes a lot of things. Many people are powerful and people do not like them. We say that if you do not respect Lakshmi Ji, she will leave your house. In the same way, power comes and goes. So, we have to be humble.

Sadaf Khan: The biggest thing is that you haven't seen the future, even the greatest kings had died in a pit and some poor people have lived a very beautiful life even in a hut.

I want to share a small thing here. I love tea and even when I get a little time, I drink tea, not from an expensive place but a small stall where I go every time, it is near Amity.

Rajesh Aggarwal: Please call me there next time (laughing).

Sadaf Khan: Sure sir. So, sir, there's a family who sells tea at that stall. There are three kids, a husband, and a wife. I watch them every time, they become very happy while sharing small things with each other, like when their mother is cooking something they all sit around. I have interacted so much with them that whenever they make snacks they even share them with me too.

When prasad comes on Tuesday, I get it too. So, you don't need to be popular when you are famous, if you are humble then also you can be popular among others.

Question 6

Sadaf Khan: Basically if I ask this question. I would like to ask Rajesh Sir first to respond and then I will come to Joe sir. If we see today there is money, power, and our life. Is it possible to balance all of these? Is it possible for us to earn good money, get popular with humbleness and do humanitarian things? I want to know the ground reality. Mostly everyone shares on their social platforms that they are investing a part of their earnings somewhere. Maybe it is due to tax savings. But I want to ask if it is possible if someone wants to do this from the heart? A person who has a lot of money and a lot of humanity too.

I want to add that a person can probably do all this in the beginning or start but how to continue it or keep going on?

Rajesh Aggarwal: Sadaf, I want to share an incident which occurred yesterday only. Maybe this can justify it. Yesterday, when we sat for dinner, my wife and daughter saw an ant in the curd. My wife told my daughter to take out that ant and do that in a way the ant can survive as it was still alive. This is a very small incident that happened in 5 seconds. I was watching with appreciation and I was feeling proud that I am very fortunate to have this family with me who knows how to appreciate everything.

My opinion in this is if we have this upbringing, like Dodani Sir has given great teaching to his kids, if we have such an upbringing and a good education then this money and fame is just a passing phase. It comes, you use it and it goes away, you should not lose that humanity. Somewhere I think as this is the last question, if we go to heaven, God will ask for the humbleness that I sent, did you bring it back more or brought arrogance back. Based on that only, you will get heaven or hell. This is what comes to my mind. These are some of my thoughts about the question you asked.

Sadaf Khan: This is a very beautiful answer. I think Jawahar Sir will teach a lot in this question as the things he said in the previous question were very motivating and spiritual. The greatest thing about all these five sessions is that whether we discussed money, popularity, Buddha, or Love but we had that spiritual essence in all those sessions and that is very important for all of us. So, I would like to hear Joe sir's views now.

Jawahar Dodani: You know, I will talk about my personal experience. I am very fortunate, my mom believed in God. I think I have her blessings. I challenged myself, God, and my mother that whatever I am and the things I face, if there is a change after getting money or power then please take me away from this world before that happens. This is my humble request to God. I even told my friends if you ever think that there is some change in me, please let me know.

I will take this opportunity to tell a bit of my life history. Before coming to the US, I was 27 and I have been here for 39 years, I am

66 now. This December it will be 40 years of being in the US. I have gone through various phases in my life up and down. I did a lot of things. During 2005-06, I was a millionaire, I had a house of 8000 sq. feet, and there were 7 bedrooms, a swimming pool, and everything. During 2007-08, I went completely down, so much so that I to file bankruptcy. I had to do three jobs just to run the house. I never thought that I got any changes during the period when I was a millionaire and when I did three jobs together. I did a job as a waiter, I worked for Uber and I took orders from guests. God again started giving me money. I am the same human who has one nose, two ears, and two eyes but somehow I earned money due to some reasons. It was probably my hard work, my skills, and sometimes through my luck or maybe my mother's blessings too. So, I don't think there is any difference in me. That is my personal opinion. I ask my heart if there are any changes in me and I don't think that happened.

So, I pray to god for this thing only that yes I want to be world-famous, if I wouldn't become world-famous then please let me be happy. If I become world-famous then don't change me. The way I am talking to Sadaf and Rajesh Sir and other people, I want to be like this only. It doesn't matter if I become famous or not. I don't want myself to be sad if I do not become famous. This is my prayer to God and my mother. I would ask the audience to bless me and my mother to bless me. I don't want to change. The last day when I leave this world, whether I become famous or not, I want to be the same as I am today. This is my only wish.

Sadaf Khan: Sir, this was beautiful. I just want to say that I have known you for the last 7 months. I will say you are one of the most humble people I have ever met. Rajesh Sir, I tell everyone that the person who teaches you when he talks with you in a good way matters the most. And whenever sir talks about whether he is tired or busy, you can feel that he is always positive and he gives life lessons too. So, this is a very big thing to me. The people who know you personally or professionally will say this, you are Heart To Heart Conversation and you are proving it. Thank You.

❑